The Insider's Guide to Real Estate

By Adam Williams

TABLE OF CONTENTS

INTRODUCTION

The goal of this ebook is to help you discover some of the **_secrets_** in real estate that the average person is not aware of. Knowing these secrets – or tricks – or inside scoop – _whatever_ you want to call it, will give you that edge and turn you into a smart investor.

You see, real estate is one activity where curiosity does NOT kill the cat. The more you're curious about the business of selling and buying property, the <u>better</u> will be your grasp of the mysteries that only a select few have unravelled through their diligence and hard work. Many of them will not share these mysteries with you...because they're worried that you might cut into their slice of the profit pie.

Untold fortunes have been made in real estate; it would not be surprising if during the last 5-7 years, some ordinary mortals have become instant millionaires, thanks to the feverish upswing in the industry.

The world of real estate has changed; people are now considering going into it as one of the sure fire ways to a golden future.

So...we ask: how do they do it?

For a few, it's *sheer luck*, given the recent real estate boom; for most others, however, it's that they have **legal inside knowledge** – the kind that *outsiders* are not privy to. Success coaches and motivators will tell you that to be successful in any endeavour – real estate included – you must get the **TOTAL** picture, not just half of it. You must get to know the **TWO SIDES OF THE COIN**, and discover a hidden third side, if there's one.

This **insider's guide to real estate** ebook therefore you provides guiding principles that you can tap to your advantage.

You'll get the whole piece of pie, not just a half-baked tart (no pun intended), the two to three sides of the coin, or both ends of the spectrum, if you will.

So we searched far and wide to get into the minds of not only sellers but also buyers and real estate brokers. We'll also throw in some facts on the financing options in real estate.

This ebook is organized into five sections:

  o **Section 1:   Know your Buyers**

  o **Section 2:   From Agent/Broker to Real Estate Professional**

You can, if you wish, read this ebook from cover to cover; and for some readers, this will be the most valuable approach.

However, if you're already a little real estate *savvy*, you can easily jump to a particular category and glean the wisdom that you're currently lacking. Furthermore, long after you've finished reading this ebook (or reading sections that are relevant to your needs), this ebook will serve you as an *invaluable* reference tool.

We've searched **behind the hype** to uncover the guiding principles that drive success in real estate selling.

Remember, please: markets boom and wane; certain types of properties (such as condos) can be hot one year, while rental properties can be hot in another. From a distance, real estate is one of the most dynamic and changing fields there is.

Yet inside that change is a core *wisdom* that remains constant. Successful real estate sellers, from the millionaire in the car next to you as you drive, to Donald Trump, **know what these principles are**.

And by the time you've finished reading this ebook, you'll know them too. And while, yes, the markets will always change, you'll be confident, calm, focused, and it is our hope and expectation: financially successful!

PART 1: KNOW YOUR BUYERS!

As you know, aside from food and clothing, shelter is a fundamental need. People need a roof over their heads, a place they can call home.

Now, this may seem like obvious information and not important for us to think about, but really, it's a *very* important thing to be aware of as you sell your real estate. Why?

Because this awareness points to one essential fact that should give you an ENORMOUS amount of confidence; especially if this is going to be your very first (of many!) real estate sales transactions: there will always be people looking for houses, regardless of whether we live in good times or bad. **Knowing the types of buyers in the market will help your position as a seller!**

The Buyer Pool

So who are these buyers that are poised to do business with you? They are people in your *buyer pool*. The phrase "buyer pool" refers to those people who are interested in buying a certain piece of property in a certain location at a certain price. This is the group that you, as a seller, should focus on. The buyer pool is different from the bunch of mere onlookers or "prowlers" who like to spend Sunday afternoons looking into the homes of other people.

As you gain experience in this field, you'll almost instantly be able to tell the genuine buyers from the speculators (or the people who are just bored and like looking at real estate...and yes, there are some of them out there).

Bill Effros, in his great book *How to Sell Your Home in 5 Days,* says the profile of a buyer pool will **change** constantly. Some buyers may decide eventually to purchase a home elsewhere, some get frustrated and leave the pool; still others decide they want to buy and therefore stay in the pool.[1]

The buyer pool is made up of different types of buyers – bear in mind that some buyers are looking for homes NOT to live in, but to invest in. You will typically encounter a mix of the following types of buyers:

> **End buyers**: buyers who will live in the home.

> **Professional buyers** – these include real estate brokers, builders who want to develop real estate in your location, speculators (quick cash wheelers

---

[1] Bill Effros. How to Sell Your Home in 5 Days. Workman Publishing, New York, 1998.

and dealers) and developers looking to buy strictly for the land value. Effros says not to be afraid of professional buyers. If circumstances warrant, they could offer the best price for your house, given their cash reserves.

- **Cash buyers** – this is the group to whom you can consider giving a discount because you do away with the lending and mortgage nitty gritty that could take weeks, even months. Cash is king, so flexibility in negotiating price is not a bad idea.

- **Mortgage buyers** – since majority of people can't buy homes for cash, they borrow the funds to acquire possession of a piece of property. They fall into two groups:

  1. the pre-qualified ones (those who have started the process and have discussed preliminary details with the bank);
  2. pre-approved mortgage buyers (the bank has made a commitment to lend them a specific amount of money under certain terms and conditions).[2]

---

[2] Bill Effros. How to Sell Your Home in 5 Days. Workman Publishing, New York, 1998.

The Buyer's Perspective

Selling your house quickly and successfully requires that you see a piece of property through a *"buyer's eyes"*. How do you do this? Well, put yourself in the buyer's shoes. What does he/she see about your house that you haven't noticed yourself?

One real estate broker said that a trick she's learned in getting sellers to think "out of the box" is to take them across the street from their house, and then asks them to give their house a long hard look, and spot things they've never noticed before.

When this exercise is done, she then takes them on a detailed tour of their house: front yard, back yard, side alleys, garage, bathrooms, the whole look-see. This way, they come up with a list of repair jobs that need to be done before they can even think of putting their house on the market.

What Buyer's Look For

What do buyers look for in terms of the house itself? Many agree that location is a decisive factor, but so are tangibles like the price and condition of the property (is the price worth the additional huge sums of money to put this house back into mint condition? How much time will I need to renovate the dilapidated portions of this house?). Buyers will be on the alert for the following:

Start with the **<u>outside</u>** of the house and ask yourself the following questions – because these are the questions that your potential buyer will be asking!:

⇨ Do these garbage cans, discarded wood scraps and building materials   strewn about carelessly an indication of the seller's negligence?

⇨ Are the gutters and roof in place? When was the last time the seller changed the roof?

⇨ Apart from the human occupants of the house, are there termites and other insects that live here also?

⇨ These overgrown bushes and trees are distracting. What is it that the sellers don't want us to see?

⇨ Is the lawn is looking unhealthy? Is the rest of the house like that?

⇨ Have the patios and decks been converted into storage areas? Why can't we see what they actually look like?

⇨ The paint is peeling off; is that why the house looks so drab and uninviting?

⇨ Why are there no lights outside the house? Is this the owner's way of saving on utility bills? Is this a safe neighbourhood?

The above questions are just a few of the many questions buyers are likely to ask with respect to the outside of the house. A house's exterior constitutes the buyer's first impression. And we all know what they say about first impressions – they are powerful and outweigh other considerations![3]

Now let's look at the **<u>inside</u>** the house: what are buyers looking at?

Barb Schwarz advises sellers to be guided by the 3 C's in real estate:

1. cleanliness
2. clutter
3. color

These three are self-explanatory, yet many sellers overlook the fact that buyers have fixed ideas about what makes a house clean, bright and uncluttered. Don't take clutter for granted. **Clutter is a big turnoff**. Too many objects lying around the house collect dust, and when you

---

[3] Barb Schwarz. How to List Residential Estate Successfully. Prentice Hall, New Jersey. 1991.

have an open house and the sun is streaking in through those large windows, the dust becomes very conspicuous.

Schwarz explains: "Clutter makes it difficult for a purchaser to _mentally move into_ a home". This means that purchasers have a hard time imagining where their sofas and entertainment centers will be placed because the clutter is hampering visualization.

This is what Schwarz tells her clients: "the way you live in a home and the way you sell a home are two different things". This is just her way of saying that some clutter does give a home a lived-in feeling, but too much is too much and makes buyers very, very nervous.

Respect Your Buyers' Intelligence!

Never underestimate the intelligence of buyers even if they strike you as inexperienced, first time buyers. Since governments have stepped into the domain of real estate, they are now warning home buyers about potential environmental dangers lurking inside houses. So what aspects of home buying are governed by regulations? Ilyce Glink warns that most professional house inspectors are not qualified to do special tests for toxic substances, although more and more individuals are specializing in these types of home testing.[4]

- **_Radon_** – the US government reported in 1989 that radon was the cause of 22,000 deaths per year and that it is the second leading cause of lung cancer in the US after cigarette smoking. Radon is an odourless, natural gas that comes from the earth and seeps through cracks in the house or its foundation.

- **_Asbestos_** – Glink says that if your home was built after 1980, there is no need to worry about asbestos. This is a microscopic fiber that escapes to the air and is ingested by humans through their noses and mouths. Buyers who have lingering fears about asbestos may demand a written report stating that the house is asbestos-free.

- **_Lead_** – Paints and water can contain high levels of lead that are harmful, particularly to children. Their physical and mental development is affected when they are exposed to this substance. Lead paint and lead in water are usually found in older homes (pre 70's). Pipes in older homes for example that were soldered together with lead can transmit lead particles into the water system.

---

[4] Ilyce R. Glink. 100 Questions Every Home Seller Should Ask. Times Books (Random House). USA. 1995.

PART 2: FROM REAL ESTATE BROKER/AGENT TO REAK ESTATE PROFESSIONAL

If your goal is to sell your house at **well over** the price you asked for and for the whole transaction to be hassle-free from A to Z, then perhaps you should start __thinking__ like a real estate broker or agent.

During times when the real market is rollicking to new, unimaginable heights, and you hear of brokers pocketing enormous amounts of commissions and fees making them millionaires overnight, you'd like to know, deep down in your heart, what makes them tick. This new crop of wealth builders is making everyone envious, including you.

And here you are – all you really want is to learn the tricks to sell your house **successfully**. Learn from the pros. What makes the pros stand out and the mediocre drop out later in the game? Get inside the mind of the real estate professional and think like him. Who knows, after you do sell your house successfully, you may decide to be a broker yourself, having learned the pitfalls and felt the glory of just this one deal.

Tom Hopkins talks about the true professionals:

"**Professionals are highly goal-oriented. They strive for a certain number of homes listed and sold each month, a certain income, a trophy, or an award. They know exactly what they're looking for and when they'll achieve it...you see, the successful ones, the true professionals, begin where the failures stop. They do what the failures are afraid or too lazy to do.**"[5]

Attitude is Everything!

A positive attitude tops the list of characteristics that real estate professionals live by. When the world comes crumbling down, as in a depressed real estate cycle, they look at downturns as an opportunity and maximise on that opportunity.

Professionals make every effort to let their image speak for their success: The trappings of success must convey

---

[5] Tom Hopkins, Mastering the Art of Selling Real Estate. Penguin Group. USA. 2004.

your competence in the field. Do your car, briefcase, desk and office communicate a successful business career?

Professionals have an organised and efficient follow-up system. Their success at closing deals depends on returning calls, prioritizing appointments, punctuality and integrity. This is the only way people will entrust the sale of their homes to them. The client's comfort level is important to a professional - an element he never takes for granted.

A real estate professional stays in tune. He reads the classified ads religiously, and makes it his business to know what's going on. His networking skills are above average, he attends the latest seminars, nurtures close relationships with people who are directly or indirectly connected to the real estate industry:

- Contractors
- Builders
- Developers
- Bankers
- insurance companies
- settlement agents
- trustees
- other brokers

Reach out and see people. Hopkins says: "There are literally thousands of people in your area who need and deserve professional assistance with their real estate needs. If you don't take it to them, they might be short-changed by someone less professional. The more people you can meet, the more you can serve."[6]

The Steps to Being a Professional

Successful real estate selling is based on being well-informed about the hidden strategies of the trade. If you do decide that you want to be a real estate professional – a profession that will most likely bring you into the inner sanctum of the cult, how do you get started?

Apart from taking the usual course and getting licensed, Tom Hopkins believes you should take the following steps:

- ✓ Have a professional photograph taken. Clients like to put a face to the name, especially the person they picked to sell their house.

- ✓ Get a cell phone with voice mail. This is indispensable, if you want to return calls promptly.

---

[6] Tom Hopkins.

- ✓ Purchase a good computer with a high processor capacity, and get your hands on software such as ACT!, Goldmine or Top Producer.

- ✓ Get email. Who doesn't need an email address these days? Surveys show that less than 6% of real estate agents with email check their mail twice a day. Be ahead of the pack.

- ✓ Get Internet – be familiar with thousands of resources dedicated to the real estate industry: industry news, training opportunities, public records, lead generation, etc. Be sure you have Mapquest (you don't want to waste time figuring out how to get to a particular address).

- ✓ Have a digital camera handy. You'll want to produce quality photographs of the properties you're selling. And don't forget to have business cards printed.

About Doubts...

Some individuals have doubts about a real estate

professional's competence when they're just starting out. Experience is, after all, the old reliable – in any profession, not just in real estate.

 But the true, beginning professionals don't let this long-held belief discourage them. They are usually able to demonstrate, quite skilfully, that they are the hungriest and the most willing to do whatever it takes to sell a house.

Enthusiasm and zeal go a long way – two traits that older professionals sometimes take for granted because they've been in the business long enough to develop a subtle smugness.

SECTION 3: ON THE PROWL FOR HOT PROPERTIES!

"Hot shots" is the name given to jackpot properties that every person who dabbles in real estate part time or full time watches out for. They keep their eyes and ears open to potential deals and jump at the first opportunity as soon as they know that the jackpot property is in the market. Their gut instincts tell them that this property will generate handsome dividends if the deal is handled properly.

Separating the Good from the Bad

Being able to discern the difference between a good and bad piece of property usually comes with insider knowledge and long years of active duty in the real estate battlefield. One writer calls real estate an emotional business. One manifestation of this is that buyers are easily swayed by the appearance of the building or its fantastic location.

But Tyler Hicks says that "buying the wrong real estate...can be a mistake. You really won't be penalized for life. But you may have a few years of tight money.

That's why it's important that *every* piece of real estate you buy be a good 'fit' for you."[7]

Finding Hot Properties

Be on the lookout for re-negotiated real estate deals, what Tyler calls the "**real estate workouts**". These are deals where lenders, so as not to foreclose on a property, extend the term of the mortgage loan so that monthly payments and terms are easier for individuals. This is how the real estate pros lay their hands on properties about to be foreclosed because the property is being sold below market price.

Want to have fun and get educated at the same time? Attend local **property auctions**. This is more for networking purposes and to get potential leads from others who make it a business to attend these auctions religiously. If one leading broker likes you, he/she may steer you to the right deals.

Keep a roving eye on **government assistance programs**, specifically those geared towards affordable housing programs for seniors and low income families. As governments become more sensitive to the needs of

---

[7] Tyler G. Hicks. How to Make Big Money in Real Estate in the Tighter, Tougher 90's Market. Prentice Hall. USA. 1992.

aging populations, they establish housing priorities for those in most need.

Remember that populations everywhere are aging! Seniors will be in a better position to demand more services, and housing is a top priority. Real estate professionals turn these opportunities into a gold mine because of easier financing terms.

Another technique for zeroing in on jackpot properties is to explore **tax foreclosure certificates**. This is a good way of making money from good properties without actually owning the real estate. These certificates can be bought from local tax authorities for properties on which owners have not paid property taxes.

Hicks points out, "Once you own one of these low-cost certificates, you have the right to wheel and deal to sell the property to others, take it over, or otherwise make money from it. It's another way to move in on jackpot properties with small cash outlays that can make you rich – soon!"[8]

Read your newspaper everyday and look for bargains. When sellers are on the point of giving up, they transfer their ad from the national paper to the community paper, as a last ditch effort. This is another area where you can tap another hot shot.

---

[8] Tyler Hicks.

Leasing instead of Selling...

Lease with option to buy: a lease option has a longer term than a straight option, usually running for as long as one year or longer. Some will even stretch to three years, depending on the whim of the seller. While your lease is ongoing, you can rent out the property and be in a positive cash flow. The second advantage is, the property is appreciating in value. If you have a long lease option, you can then sell the property for the highest price you can obtain.

One last strategy for hot picks: be on the alert for long leases. Long leases will ensure that a property will be rented or leased for long periods of time, not just a year. Some commercial leases for example go for as long as 5 or 10 years. One example is the government. Take post offices as the best illustration. The government will usually rent space for post offices on a long term basis. If the property you are eyeing has government outlets like the post office, the automobile insurance board or the government-sponsored health centres, these buildings qualify as hot property!

LOCATION!

You've heard about the three principal parameters in real estate? One - location, two - location, and three - location. Take that with a capital "L". One trick in looking for that pot of gold at the end of the rainbow is to buy the worst property in the best neighbourhood, NOT the best property in the worst neighbourhood.

This is a cardinal rule that sophisticated inventors try never to break. Robert Allen gets the message across:

> **"If you buy the worst property in the best neighbourhood, at least you have the chance to upgrade the property to match the standards of the neighbourhood, and your property value will increase. In a bad area, your property will only decline in value along with the rest of the neighbourhood. Remember, you're buying a neighbourhood, not just a property."**[9]

A Model of Selling Success

Robert Allen's concentric circle theory makes for intelligent hunting for hot properties. The circle has a small circle in the middle called the "center."

The circles around it are identified as A, B, C, and D – A being closest to the center. The theory works this way: compare real estate to student housing. The nearer the student apartment is to campus, the higher the rent is

---

[9] Robert G. Allen. Nothing Down for the 90's. Simon & Schuster. New York. 1990.

and the lower the turnover is. That student apartment therefore – being in circle A is a good investment. The same applies to houses. Which neighbourhoods are nearer to centers of employment, education, shopping and conveniences? Try to hunt for properties in the A circle, and avoid those in the D area.

Introducing the Don't Wanter

Don't-wanters are people who will give anything to sell their property, to be rid of it completely, and who cross their fingers every minute hoping a seller will buy their property. Because of this, they can be flexible as you want them to be. How many of them are don't-wanters? "Even in extremely tight sellers' markets, there are still plenty of don't-wanters. Perhaps 5% of all sellers are willing to be flexible enough to be called don't-wanters. Some new investors get discouraged early because they haven't learned that 95% of the sellers are not flexible. They need to be dealing with the 5% who are don't-wanters."[10]

---

[10] Robert G. Allen.

SECTION 4: COMMON SELLING MISTAKES

Here's some very useful advice: **don't treat your real estate agent as Mr. or Ms. Know it All**. They are **not** infallible!

Believe it or not, they don't know everything there is to know about real estate. They make mistakes, just like everyone. When an agent tells you to wait because your property will probably not sell these days, take her/his word with a grain of salt. Question motives!

➤ Is she/he trying to get you to lower your price so she/he can sell it much quicker, thus pocketing the commission quicker?

➤ Is she/he concentrating on other higher priced homes in the area and hence has no time for you?

Sellers often make the mistake of believing their agents. One such seller was so disgusted because she/he allowed the agent to let her take her house off the listing. The agent kept telling her to wait some more. Three years later, her property was still unsold, and in her frustration, decided to go with another agent.

Investigate Credentials

Once you've signed a contract with an agent that the house is exclusively hers to sell, you could be stuck with an inefficient agent for a long time. Before you sign on the dotted line, investigate your agent's credentials.

Ask for the names of other sellers she's worked for, and where possible, speak to these past clients and ask them whether or not they were satisfied with her service. Check out qualifications, licence and board certifications. Some sellers make the mistake of engaging the services of an agent in a hurry because they're eager to sell.

As Gregory Lerch stressed, hire a real estate like you would an attorney or accountant. Try to distinguish the full time professionals from the part-timers – those who occasionally dabble in real estate, who get into the business of selling homes only when they need quick cash.[11]

Have Reports In-Hand

---

[11] Gregory Lerch. How to Sell Your Home When Homes Aren't Selling. Betterway Publications, Inc. Virginia, USA. 1991.

Another mistake sellers make is not having written inspection reports to show to prospective buyers. The regulations about asbestos, radon and lead are fairly stringent and must follow governmental guidelines. Ensure that professional house inspectors have the capability – and certification – to do these tests.

Know the Rules...

Sellers often decide to go solo without enlisting the help of an agent for the sole purpose of being able to save thousands of thousands in agent's commissions. This is a legitimate reason.

If you do decide to sell your house on your own, make sure you know the rules of the game like the back of your hand. Have it down pat.

> **The second, even bigger mistake, is that some sellers don't have the ability and understanding to know when to quit as independent sellers!**

If your house is still in the market for a year, even if other homes are selling like hotcakes in the neighbourhood, then it's time to take a step back and see what you're doing wrong. A real estate agent may be your alternative.

According to Lerch, "market studies have shown that you can actually lose money when your home sits on the market for an extended period. Knowing that, your goal should be either to learn how to extend your optimum selling period or market your home so it sells within the time limits the market has dictated".[12]

[12] Gregory Lerch.

Be Zone Conscious

If you don't keep up with your city hall urban planners and engineers, you could be selling your house just before zoning adjustments are being implemented. These zoning adjustments could considerably increase the value of your property. Haste makes waste, they say. So keep your eyes and ears tuned to municipal changes that could enhance (or affect) your position as a seller.

Pricing Too High? Too Low?

High and low pricing: sellers who like to make a killing price their property way too high, making it out of reach to buyers who are looking at similar properties in the same location. Don't be priced out. Going to the other end of the spectrum, you'll know that you priced your house too low when it's bought the same or next day after you or your agent advertised it. It was "snatched" by someone else because it was way below market price.

Obviously, you as seller will try to get the highest price you can get for your property so you start with a high price.

The buyer, on the other hand, will offer the lowest possible price he can negotiate. So you start high and he starts low. This creates plenty of room to negotiate – the gray area that lies between the highest and lowest prices.

This is where sellers can make the mistake of not demonstrating sufficient flexibility to the buyer!

This is the reason there are high and low prices in real estate – what Albert Lowry called practising the give-and-take principle. "Such give-and-take is part of the bargaining process...It gives you both room to negotiate...As you and the buyer make proposals and counterproposals, you are inching closer to agreement...Then at some point one of you will yield no further."[13] Develop the extra sense to know when to stop negotiating.

Some More Common Selling Mistakes

Ilyce Glink names a few more mistakes sellers make:

----

[13] Albert J. Lowry. How You Can Become Financially Independent by Investing in Real Estate. Simon & Schuster. New York. 1982.

- **Undefined motivation** – are you selling your house because you want to or have to? Honesty in answering this question will affect your negotiation abilities. You might be sending the wrong messages to your agent or buyer. If you and your husband have mixed feelings, be sure you iron out your differences and reasons for selling before putting your house in the market.

- **Hanging around during open houses**. If you have an agent, let her do the work. Don't make buyers uncomfortable by your presence. They may want to ask the agent certain questions that they don't necessarily want you to hear.

- **Pets and Odours** – some buyers may not exactly be animal lovers; other buyers are turned off by cooking smells. Keep the pets invisible, and the smells at bay with air freshener.

- **Letting the house go stale** – if your house has been on the ads too long, know when to pull it out. Don't give buyers the chance to "suspect" something is wrong with your house. Take out the for sale sign and come back another time.

- **Timing**: when sellers sell their house in hopes to buy another, they fail to recognize proper timing as an essential component of the real estate process. When their offer on the new house is accepted but there are no firm buyers for their old house, they are forced to apply for a bridge loan which can make them out of pocket for a few years. Wait until your house is sold, or at least wait before a firm offer is in your hands.

> **Mortgage payments:** just because your house is sold does not mean you can skip mortgage payments. Make sure your mortgage payments are up to date until closing. When closing documents are drawn up, the lender will take any unpaid amounts and deduct them from any monies due to you. Check with your lawyer, escrow or title company officer.

➤ **Deposit money**: there is no fixed standard practice regarding deposit money – sometimes called "earnest" money. Requiring a deposit from the buyer is simply the seller's need for assurance that the buyer will buy the property and has the financing required to buy the property. When time and money are spent in the showing, negotiation and contract preparation procedures, the seller has to be compensated for lost opportunities to sell to someone else if the original committed buyer suddenly backs out of the deal. Don't omit discussing this with your agent or settlement agent. It's added protection for you as seller.

SECTION 5: FINANCING

When it comes to borrowing money, banking institutions will have set criteria for mortgages and profiles of individuals that they will lend the money to. Many full-service banks will provide complete financing, but they don't necessarily tell you everything. So you may have to do some of the homework yourself instead of relying 100% on these lending institutions. They will structure a loan that is most lucrative to them.

Construction/permanent loans

This is one way of financing a real estate purchase. A construction loan is a loan package consisting of two loans in one. The first one is to enable borrowers to purchase all the materials needed to build the house. When the house is finished, the loan is converted into a typical permanent loan. A closing takes place before any monies are released by the bank. So you and the bank will have to agree to a fixed amount prior to any closing or any withdrawals.

EXAMPLE: Say you need $250,000. After closing, you need to withdraw an amount to pay for the land. The bank releases the funds. Then you'll need to funds to buy the construction materials and pay for the contractor's time. How many withdrawals you can make and at what intervals vary from one institution to another. When the house nears completion, you take one final amount to pay for the rest of the bills. The final amount you pay, say $200,000.00 out of the $250,000.00 you originally borrowed, can be converted into a permanent loan.

Since construction loans are interest only loans, **remember that the principal is <u>not</u> paid monthly along with the interest!** You will receive a monthly bill for the interest on the outstanding balance. Chris Condon recommends two techniques you can use:[14]

1. do not overestimate the loan amount. Borrowers pay "points" on the loan. In the previous example, you used only $200K out of the $250K. This can represent a waste of money because you could be paying points on money you'd never use.

2. draw the right amount. Bank inspectors will usually make inspections of the house to verify whether the amounts you have drawn are justified. Most construction loans allow a certain number of free inspections before they start charging for the inspection. The trick is to decide which is more expensive to you: the interest fee or the inspection fee. Chris Condon advises exploring the possibility of taking smaller but more frequent draws.

Permanent Mortgage Loan

---

[14] Chris Condon. Building Real Estate Riches. McGraw Hill. USA. 2004.

Many types of permanent mortgage loans exist. Not all options are available with a construction/permanent loan so ask the right questions. Monthly payments include principal and interest. Types of permanent loans are:

Conventional Loans

Conventional loans – any permanent, long-term financing that does not fall under VA or FHA.

VA Loans

These provides veterans with access to loans not requiring a down payment. It's the VA that acts as guarantor.

FHA Loans

To eliminate the lender's risk, Federal Housing Administration provides lenders with an insurance policy. This helps to offset any fees tied to any of the usual lender's risks.

Fixed and Adjustable Mortgages and Loans

Fixed rate mortgage – loans are amortized over a period of 10, 15, 25 or 30 years. Interest rate is constant for the term of the loan.

Adjustable rate mortgage – also knows as the variable rate loan; interest rate is calculated on the basis of prime rate set by the Federal Reserve. If prime rate goes down, your monthly payments go down, if they go up, so do your principal/interest payments.

Home equity loan – when you've built enough equity on your house; i.e. it is 75% paid for, you can borrow funds against this equity to pay for renovations in the hopes of an eventual sale. Banks' terms and conditions on home equity loans vary, so speak to your lender about the ramifications of the home equity loan.

Reverse mortgage – some banks will actually try to convince you to do a reverse mortgage. Details are too cumbersome to discuss here, but speak to your bankers. It is not for everyone.

Seller Financing?

Another type of financing is suggested by Ilyce Glink called *seller financing*. It means that you, the seller, lend the money to the buyer to buy your home, thus becoming the buyer's bank. If seller and buyer agree to the logistics of seller financing, it can be a wonderful arrangement for both parties.

The advantages to the buyer include:

- ✓ quick and easy loan approval

- ✓ competitive interest rate

- ✓ lower fees than banks and other institutions usually charge

- ✓ less paperwork

The advantages to the seller include:

- ✓ equity in your home turns into an investment from which you can earn a stable rate of return

- ✓ the loan is secured by an asset – your own house

IMPORTANT: One disadvantage, however:

If the buyer defaults on the payments, you will need to bring legal action to get either your money or house back.[15]

More about Seller Financing

If you decide to go with seller financing, you should be able to spot the good candidates, just like banks do with people who apply for a loan. Borrowers should provide the following data:

---

[15] Ilyce Glink.

- their name, address, Social Security number, three previous addresses, employer's name/address/phone number

- how long they have been at their present employer, as well as the names and numbers of their last 3 employers

- a copy of their latest federal and state tax returns,

- year-to-date statement showing income, assets and liabilities,

- copies of their most recent pay stub (if you believe this is necessary),

- they must sign an agreement for you to obtain a credit report on them.

Tips for Real Estate Loan Applications

If you're applying for a real estate loan, here are some tips from Hicks that come in handy:

☑ never submit a handwritten application. Professionalism will make lenders more comfortable

☑ ensure that the loan amount you seek is appropriate to the lender.

☑ find out from the channel what the debt cover ratio is for income properties, so that you can position your approach. Ten years ago, the acceptable ratio was 1.5 or higher. Check this figure out as this might have changed,

☑ prepare a good real estate business plan for the property you want to buy (this applies to commercial properties). Attach this business plan with your loan application. This gives the lender the impression that you've done your homework,

☑ Have a co-signer for the loan. It adds to the comfort level of lenders.

If you're borrowing money to purchase property you **won't** be living in, muster up enough courage when it's time to approach a lender.

Bankers usually turn detective when commercial loans are on the table. Be aware that interest rates on loans for buildings that are not owner-occupied are much higher and down payments are sometimes higher than 25%.[16]

When applying for commercial loans, be prepared to answer the following questions:

☑ what is your total monthly income

☑ do you have copies of your income tax returns for the last 3 years?

☑ can you verify your down payment requirement, and

☑ have you borrowed any of your down payment?[17]

CONCLUSION

---

[16] Robert G. Allen.
[17] Robert G. Allen.

As we noted earlier in this ebook, real estate is a very dynamic field; and that's one of the reasons why some people are hesitant to explore it, and to **exploit** its profit potential.

The way to overcome this obstacle, and to realize incredible profit in real estate selling, is to understand this dynamic field from the *inside*; that is, to know the tips, techniques, and strategies that turn ordinary real estate transactions into extraordinary ones.

You, now, are one of the *insiders*.

Thanks to this ebook and your efforts, you possess information that millions of people simply don't have access to. And you can take this information with you to your current real estate deal, and indeed, to your future ones as well.

You now know the following keys:

✓ **Knowing your Buyers**

✓ **Going from Agent to *Professional***

✓ **Finding HOT Properties**

✓ **Avoiding Mistakes**

✓ **Financing Success**

Use your new information wisely and professionally, and you'll soon discover why people who enter the real estate selling game – and play it *well* – stay there for life. It's fun, exciting, always interesting, and best of all: **profitable if you're an insider – and that's what you are right now!!!**

FORECLOSURES DEMYSTIFIED

Introduction to Foreclosure

In the recent times, the concept of foreclosure has become immensely popular. In spite of the gaining popularity, there are many people who do not know about the reasons and circumstances that show the way to Foreclosures. Not only that, but people do not even know how to avoid foreclosures.

One has to have in-depth knowledge of the facts related to the foreclosures. This will give a better understanding and help people to handle situations. Like what are foreclosures? Situations leading to foreclosures, the laws related to the homeowners and money lenders, procedures to know of when one is involved in a foreclosure and more.

This is a book which will help one in understanding the different minute details involved in foreclosures and how one can avoid the same. Read on for some interesting and basic facts on foreclosure!

The real estate market has suffered a set back right from the year 2006. Since then the home owners around the globe have been forced to come to terms with foreclosures. A foreclosure is a term associated with forgoes or fail to retain the ownership rights of one's house or property. Failing to pay for the mortgage of the purchased property leads to foreclosures. Believe it or not the present economic slump is also a powerful effect of the foreclosures that have been happening over a period of time.

Simple Understanding of Foreclosure

Foreclosure is technically defined as a right of redemption on a property. The situation arises when a person has taken a loan on property by mortgaging it or has purchased the property through a loan and is not being able to pay for the repayment installments. In most cases the borrower is a house owner who had accrued his property with the aid of loans, which due to some reason he is unable to pay back in time. As soon as the borrower fails to pay the loan amount he or she becomes a "defaulter". If the defaulter has no other source to pay off for the loan, the property is seized and sold to recover the loan amount. This will result in a decrease in credit rating for the borrower who becomes a looser in the future.

A borrower can take a loan for purchase of the property from a financial institution or a bank. The sanction of the loan involves quite a few legal formalities. This results in the intervention of a third party in the cases. At this point, the judicial and non judicial foreclosures come into the picture.

Judicial foreclosures are foreclosures that are overlooked and executed by the court. In this case the lender can take over the property directly with the assistance of court intervention. The process would be conducted by the mortgagee or the agent under the guidance and surveillance of the court.

The final decision is taken by the mortgagee or lender in case of non judicial foreclosures. The foreclosure would be conducted all the way through by a public auction system. The borrower receives a notice from the sheriff in case of judicial foreclosure. The auction is conducted at the court hall. The process involves legal formalities held between the lender and the borrower. A person who is purchasing a property in an auction can make huge profits, if he can manage to buy the property at a lesser auctioned price than that of its market value.

In cases where the bank takes over the property one would have to wait till the bank finds a perfect buyer for the same. Given the facts, it can be wisely said that Foreclosures certainly aid borrowers to meet their loan arrears.

Owners of a property try to avoid the lengthy and elaborate procedures involved in Foreclosures. This is specially related to borrowers who have a history of bad credit because it will be very difficulty for them to avail loans. Though there are institutions to assist you with foreclosures yet for the interest rate can turn out to be sky high for borrowers with a bad credit history. One can purchase a relatively high priced property at a low cost at foreclosure auctions or sale. This is seen as an advantage for the buyers. The purchaser of the foreclosed property can then sell off the same at a profit making and titanic gains!

Situations Leading to Foreclosures

When no further monetary dealings are possible between the borrower and the lender, proceedings for Foreclosures commences. When borrower is entirely bankrupt, he can find no alternative to repay the loans he had taken for his or against his property. Then, he is left with no other choice apart from the Foreclosure.

Foreclosures do not give anyone the consent to throw you out of the house without prior notice. Only when there is judicial intervention, the court can order you to leave your house. The court too has a set of rules for foreclosures and evictions which must be followed.

When the foreclosure of your property is handled by a bank, it is recommended for you to find out from the bank as to when they will begin the procedures for the same. It may as long as 90 days for the bank to commence with the proceedings. It is best to have the knowledge of the dates of proceedings, so that you can make alternative arrangements to move out in that span of time. This is because you will have to find a house which you like and fits within your rent budget and then move out your belongings.

Foreclosure proceedings begin when a borrower skips the mortgage and all other associated payments related to the owned property. A bank will first try and work out a solution with the borrower so that the foreclosure can be avoided. Banks are known to make settlements or find alternative methods prior to the decision of the foreclosure. When the borrower continues to miss the payments and avoids contact, the bank will resort to legal action. It will first send a note to the borrower demanding payment, based on the acceleration clause. The acceleration clause is a kind of mortgage note. It reads that upon failure to make the repayments the total amount which is due on the borrower will have to be paid in total at call. It would also include the amount of interest calculated by the bank as per the terms of the contract.

Once you receive the mortgage note from the bank, it is indication enough that you should contact your attorney. An attorney will help you to proceed with your legal formalities regarding the foreclosure. A mortgage note is the starting point of a future foreclosure. The banks would follow up by sending across the "Notice of Intent to foreclose" the notice is served with the help of the sheriff and the court.

Once the notice is served it is expected from the borrower to meet up with the authorities and work out a solution. When the borrower does not respond to any notice or call the borrower will be tagged guilt of missing payments by the court. The court will apparently give legal permission to the bank to then begin the proceedings of foreclosure. The bank then announces the foreclosure of the property in the local media through advertisement. An auction is followed on the decided date and the property is handed to the highest bidder. The borrower loses his property as the price for his loan.

Contingencies Taking Towards Foreclosure

When a borrower misses to make repayments for his amount of loan, it will lead to foreclosure of the property. The specified number of missed payments which would lead to seal on the borrower's property is mentioned in the loan contract.

The number of defaulted payments also depends on the characteristics of loan you have along with the contract terms. The mortgage contract states clearly as to how many payments you can miss ahead of a Notice of Default is filed against you.

As and when a person misses the first payment of the loan, it is a big indication that in the future there could be a situation of foreclosure. A home equity credit line to lock your interest rates must be set to prevent such a situation. This will give you the prospect to get fast cash in cases of emergency.

Missing paying up a mortgage payment not as simple as missing a credit card payment. It could be counted similar to a criminal offence. After you have missed a maximum of four mortgage payments, you can be assured that a Foreclosure proceeding would be started against you.

The credit history of a person is negatively affected when he evades a mortgage repayment. A bad credit history reduces the chances of getting future loans. These loans could be useful to a person as he can save his house from getting mortgaged, through the loans. If you default at the mortgage repayments, chances of your getting future loans decrease with every payments default.

Avoid missing payments in a row as this will speed up the foreclosure procedure for you. Once you have missed around three to four payments, the lender party, bank or financial institution will begin the foreclosure proceedings against you.

Parties Involved in Foreclosure

Missed payments would lead the banks or the financial institutions to declare foreclosure. Once the foreclosure has been declared the rest would follow:

- Mortgage holders and other lien holders who hold interest in loans on your property, used as collateral, would be amongst one of the first people to foreclose your property.

- Banks and additional financial institutions from where you had got a lump sum loan for your property following which you failed to pay them back the monthly installments are also liable to put up your property for a foreclosure. This will be done with assistance from the local court or judiciary.

- A forced foreclosure and eviction can be issued by the sheriff, if the homeowner fails to make the payments even after repeated warnings. Notice is even served when the borrower does not respond or ignores eviction notices.
- The property is finally foreclosed by the auction houses. Once a foreclosure has been declared, legal notices are put up in public stating the details of the property in auction. This would begin within 90 days after you have failed to make your mortgage payments and your property has been declared for foreclosures.

Relation Between Tax Lien and Foreclosure

A tax lien is imposed on a person once the property has been decided for foreclosure.

A tax lien is a type of tax imposed on property by legal institutions to secure payments of the respective taxes. These could be taxes that have been imposed on real or personal property that are a result of one failing to pay income tax or other associated taxes.

In case of Foreclosures tax liens are generally imposed

upon real estates that the property owner has to pay up under all circumstances. This tax is even imposed upon the current property owner if it was actually incurred by the prior owner of the property.

There are various methods by which tax lien related payments could be made. A property owner has the rights to make these payments directly or has the option to utilize the services of a mortgage holder via an escrow account. In case of the property owner using the services of a mortgage company, the company is liable to receive all notices related to the property and its payments and even if the property owner does not possess an escrow account, the mortgage company is bound to pay up the same in his or her behalf. However, you they have every right to demand the same from their client. In some cases the mortgage company can go as far as creating an escrow account for their clients so that they can make their payments through the same. If this is not done the mortgage company might end up making a loss in its value of mortgage lien if the taxing agency sold out the property to meet unpaid taxes foreclosure.

In cases where the property owner sells off his property before foreclosure with government aid, the tax lien if any is paid off during the closing of deal from the sale proceeds.

Tax lien comes into focus when it is not paid prior to foreclosures. In such a situation the property could be seized off and sold at a foreclosure.

For a purchaser, it becomes obligatory to check on a property that he plans to purchase especially if via foreclosures. This is to verify and check for any associated tax liens, unless he wants to fall into numerous legal clichés associated with the same. Further he will end up paying tax liens for expenses he has not incurred. He will have to pay because he purchased a property where the previous owner was a tax defaulter. In case of personal properties it becomes mandatory for the present owner to pay up all related taxes. A owner will not be permitted to sell his property unless all property related taxes have been paid by him. Every government ensures that property taxes are paid by property owners. This saves them from a tax lien being issued against them.

However, real estate owners are big time gainers when it comes to tax liens. The real estate boom that happened in recent years is in fact a result of tax liens. Properties at prime locations whose owners had failed to pay up the property taxes due to some financial crisis or personal problems led to the boom. The real estate developers who generally have a lot of money in hand make an offer to the property owners to buy property and pays off all his tax liens. This makes them the owners of prime properties at strategic locations which they can later sell at a much elevated price. All they have to do is list out such properties with tax lapse, from which they can churn out whale profits.

The Foreclosure Period

Would you like to know the amount of time required in the entire process of foreclosure? Well, this is one question that pops up in the minds of all owners involved in foreclosure. Property owners panic as to how long it will be for them from the time they take delivery of a foreclosure notice from the sheriff to the auctions to happen, and the property deal to be closed. Since they do not have the proper idea of the foreclosure period, they cannot take adequate measures to stop the property being foreclosed or chalk out other alternative plans.

Factors affecting foreclosure time period:

The duration of a foreclosure depends largely upon the governing body or state and its legal laws. The prevalent law is a vital factor that would decide when the foreclosure proceedings would start and end. This begins once the property owner has missed a mortgage payment. The property owner whose property is to be foreclosed must be aware of the same so that they are well equipped to face the situation.

Estimating time frame:

- Mortgage companies: they would generally begin the foreclosure process 3- 6 months post the owner misses the first mortgage payment.

- Though the stated period is 30 days after first missed payment, most money lenders are kind enough to provide property owners a second chance. The lenders give the owners 3-6 months time in hand to make necessary arrangements. If the loan default is paid within that period, the question of foreclosure does not come into the picture.

- Constant touch with banks: If you are a smart property owner who has fallen into a foreclosure situation, you can delay the entire foreclosure process. This can be done by being in constant contact with your bank or financial institution. This would lengthen the foreclosure procedure by months if you manage to keep your bank occupied with various paper work related to foreclosure or even make an attempt at resolving the foreclosure sale.

You can even ask your bank for extra time if you see some money coming in the future. By avoiding regular contact with the bank one would only speed up the foreclosure sale as the bank would assume that you are avoiding making of any payments.

The actual eviction from the property would only occur after the sheriff sale is over. This happens after the bank has secured a court order for eviction. This could take months to take place at times. This is to give the homeowners adequate time to relocate and plan their future. In extreme fortunate cases they can aim at refinancing or repaying their loans.

- The actual foreclosure sale would only happen two to three weeks or even months after the sheriff has declared and passed a notice. The sale of property would occur at a county courthouse which is attended by the owner too.

Importance of Having an Idea About the Time Period of Foreclosure

Most property owners who are involved in a property dispute are unaware of the exact time that they would be involved in a case their property is put up for foreclosure sale.

Since they do not have the idea of the time frame, they cannot plan any last minute actions to save their property from the foreclosure and sale. Moreover, when the sheriff plans to take quick action, the owner and family could be thrown out of the hose before they could even contemplate it.

This will just a make a person understand, how important it is to know about the time period involved in the foreclosure process. You can meet up your lawyer during that period and avoid the foreclosure by devising a plan and payments scheme.

Smart Facts to Keep Foreclosure Away

Who would like to loose his property through a foreclosure sale? Not many. It is not everyday that a person makes a house or a property. After all every body have various dreams and aspirations around their owned property. This is the very reason they would not like to simply hand it over to a third party. There may have been some financial crisis or unavoidable circumstances for which the owner may have failed to pay the mortgage loan resulting in a foreclosure. Ups and downs are a part of life. It is a sorry state of affairs but definitely not the end of the road. Well, you don't have to worry! There are numerous options slowly emerging for property owners. These are like the magic clauses which are adept in order to prevent foreclosure sale of their property.

If you have plans to avoid a foreclosure sale of your property, the first step that you ought to take is to contact your financial advisor. a legal firm which is well experienced in handling a foreclosure situation will guide you through the various options available. Apart from this you can look up different websites on the net for advises or read up blogs of people who have been victims of a foreclosure sale. You will come across some information which will give you the tips to come out of the foreclosure mess. These will give you a reasonable idea on how to advance.

As you read on, we will be giving you some *interesting tips* on how to avoid foreclosures on your property in this chapter.

Be Smart and Avoid Foreclosures?

1. To begin with *get in touch with counseling agent* to advise you for a home loan modification. A home loan modification will help you reduce your monthly EMI's for home loan. This will help you to retain your house as small monthly payments could be affordable and chances of skipping it will be less.

2. *Talk to your money lender* to help work out solutions to prevent a foreclosure. Be it your bank or any other financial institution from where you have availed the loan, speak to them for alternative ideas and plans to help you save your house. If you're unable to make your mortgage payment, get in touch with your lender immediately in order to stop foreclosure. Ignoring the bills will only make matters worse, increasing the likelihood that you'll lose your home for sure. Borrowers who look for foreclosure help early are much more likely to work out a solution, even in dire situation. Mortgage companies want to avoid foreclosure as much as you; this is because they make more money in the interest involved in the loan than they make in processing a foreclosure a deal. Based on your situation, your lender may be able to offer the foreclosure help that you require.

3. *Look for reinstatement opportunities:* in this method, the owner of the house who is apparently

also the defaulter is given another chance. He can choose to make the payments on a future date of the entire amount of loans outstanding. Who knows you can suddenly get a bulk amount from company bonus, profit or a tax refund.

4. *Go for a forbearance agreement*: That is the lender allowing the borrower to decrease or minimize the mortgage payments for a time period. Within this period options for payments are worked out on the current loan.

5. *Plan a repayment plan* with your funds lender, till you have money structured to pay your actual loan amount. This repayment plan would be so made, so that your monthly payments are made much lower and affordable. This will help you to make up most of your losses and be in a better financial position. Once you financial position improves you will to be able to pay off your loans at the actual amount once again.

6. *Mortgage modification*. Mortgage modification is the process of working out an agreement with your money lender, whereby you could request your money lender to change certain terms on your loan document. With the modification you could still pay your monthly loan amount at an affordable rate. Changes could be brought about by incorporating the amount of the missed payments into the existing loan balance. Alternatively a change in payment can by modified by altering the

interest rates from variable to be fixed. One could also extend the number of years for repaying the loan. Increasing the years would reduce the monthly loan expenditure.

7. Make sure you *opt for mortgage insurance.* Mortgage insurances are insurances issued against your loan amount which you can use in crisis situations. It can be used in the times of foreclosure whereby you could obtain some amount of money to save the present situation. An insurance claim can delay your foreclosure for months. You would qualify if your loan is between 4 and 12 months period. All you need to do is sign an interest free promissory note to enable a lien to be imposed upon your property till you are able to pay off the same. These are the numerous advantages of mortgage insurance.

8. *Avoid missing a payment* if you don't want to fall into the foreclosure trap. It's best to avoid missing a payment.

One of the finest ways to avoid a Foreclosure is to bring to a halt the filing of Notice of Default. The only way to prevent it is to be in constant touch with your money lender and not to stay away from him. Staying in touch can enable you to work out a solution. Your money lender may opt for forbearance that is by giving you adequate time to reorganize for the current situation and the default payments. In rare cases the lender can give you debt forgiveness, that is, he may forego your current payments for a time period. But it is advisable not to expect this degree of goodness. Your money lender may also extend your awaiting payments over a large period of time. When you talk to a lender in good faith, he may come up some options which may be beneficial to you. Though you cannot thank the lender enough, but you must try and meet the redesigned and comfortable pay scheme.

Don't Ignore the Situation

Ignoring will fuel the problem: that could end you up face to face with a foreclosure. Be open to negotiations and conversations with your lender at all times. Your lender would definitely work out an option for you.

Contact the State Government Housing Office for help: you can get in touch with the government housing office for any questions and information's that you would want to know regarding foreclosures. Having sufficient information about foreclosure and its connected laws will give you plenty of chance to plan a way out of this predicament situation.

Get in touch with your state housing development counselor at first. They would be bound to find a way out for you. In the United States of America there exists HUD or the Housing and Urban Development association in every state which help homeowners in times of crisis through free counseling. These counseling sessions throws light on how to avoid foreclosures. The counseling sessions are educative and helpful. They can go to the extent of explaining you every detailed law associated with foreclosures, help you plan your finance so that you could avoid the same. In some cases they could also become the intermediary between you and your money lender. This is best alternative in situations where you would not like to face each other.

Make your savings more than the expenditure: When in a crisis situation, spend only on necessities rather than luxuries and other impulse purchases. Try and cut down your everyday expenditure so that you could make your mortgage payments. When you have to make a choice between the credit card and the mortgage payment, pay for your mortgage. Remember, credit card are unsecured loans and can be settled by paying a lower price later. Cut down on restaurants, movies, outings and vacations for a time till you have made up for your losses.

Planning Your Assets

A foreclosure can be avoided if you have worked through your years to build your assets. Assets could be in the form of a car, gold or silver jewelry. Assets with high resale values, any policies, shares or savings could be used at this point of time to make your mortgage payment and save your house. Like for Christmas you could buy a policy apart from your spree shopping, for your birthday you could make some investments. All these little savings are big help when you are in a financial mess.

Take up freelancing part time jobs. If you can add an extra income by doing a part time job to meet your mortgage payment take it up! After all an extra effort can lead to an extra income that can help you avoid a foreclosure. You will, be able to save your asset with a little hard work and that too for a limited period of time. Foreclosure consultants empty promises trap: the foreclosure consultant who go outright to demonstrate to you that a foreclosure could be preventable if you remunerated them a certain amount of money. Be smart and smell the foul play.

Instead utilize that cash to pay back your mortgage loans. In fact at worst cases you could end up being a part of a foreclosure scam. These are scams that generate from profit making organizations which lure or convince you that they would avoid a foreclosure for you. No miracles happen as you see the foreclosure in front of your eyes but they are successful in extracting a heavy amount of money.

One could avoid a foreclosure when he files for a bankruptcy. This would with held foreclosure proceedings for a time period. One can make the most of this time by planning out an option as to how he will meet the loan repayment situation of the mortgage. Take help from an attorney. If you are a novice in this it would be best for you to recruit a foreclosure attorney. The attorney will direct you on how to avoid a foreclosure. He will give you the best options available to and will also come to your help with all the essential paper work necessary.

Read on the internet for various blogs and advices on how to stop a foreclosure sale. I am sure these will be helpful. You can get an occasion to relate with people who have experienced or are about to experience a foreclosure deal. There is absolutely nothing that you cannot find on the internet. The best advice on foreclosure along with practical examples will be available for you to read and understand. You can then try and imply it in your practical scenario. Use the search engines for all the help that you need.

Making Smart Money

Make smart money lender choice: One of the most important factors that could help one avoid a foreclosure is to study your money lender before you pick him or her. Not only that, but it is equally important to understand all the minute details of a loan prior to accepting it.

There is no limit to options available to stay away from a foreclosure. Abundant options can be worked out. Your alternatives don't stop unless you have given up the fight. So it is very important to be strong minded. You have to work towards a solution. Remember all the happiness you felt when you finally became the owner of the property. Think of the good times that you have spent there and those uncountable memories. All of it will give you the strength to carry on your fight to save your property. Mind the use of credit cards: You will realize that after a time you are unable to pay your mortgages because you had been busy paying off your credit card bills.

Activate home equity lines: At least 90% of foreclosures could be prohibited or delayed if home equity lines of credit were previously activated. This can often be set up for no cost and can lock in rates as low as 4%. In most cases you pay zero each month if you do not access the line. No one ever expects sudden health problems, loss of a job or emergency requiring funds fast. All of these are contingencies. These events might prevent obtaining a loan once they occur.

By setting up a home equity credit line before you ever miss a mortgage payment, you will have money when you really need it. Just write yourself a check. When things get back in order, pay back the line and then use it again the next time. But do not take advantage of it and make regular useless expenditures. It is there for times of emergencies to bail you out of financial crisis.

A friend in need is a friend indeed. In this crisis period do not forget to take help from a friend who might help you out with the money required to meet your mortgage payments. After all you can always pay a friend back that too without an interest when your sunny days arrive again! And you would not have to loose your house to a foreclosure! Do not feel ashamed to ask help from a friend, relative or close associate. After all if they really love you they would never allow you to loose your home to a disastrous thing as a foreclosure. In case you have a big ego, crush it my dear or it will crush your property.

Identify Your Issues

Face your problems: share your problems with your friends and associates and with your entire money lender. They will definitely find a solution for you. It is wise to accept that there is a problem rather than run away from it and thinking all is fine. Look for genuine money lenders: some money lender will show you no other alternative apart from the foreclosure.

They are the clan of lenders who are there only to make money and do not believe in humanitarian grounds. Remember options in 90% cases are workable so always take multiple opinions and consultations before you take a decision or are forced to take one.

Sell your property. You can yourself sell your property if you want to avoid a foreclosure. It works! Selling your home yourself will get you a higher amount rather than selling your house off through foreclosure at an auction.

This way you will definitely get more money from the sale proceeds with which you can purchase a lower or equivalent value property without having to loose out on a whole lot of money and engaging yourself in numerous paper work related to foreclosures. You can good money for your house and be saved from any sticky embarrassing situation related to foreclosure.

The last resort: even if you have lost your house or property to foreclosure you still have an option to buy it back even after you are evicted! You can end up being the highest bidder if you are able to organize the cash required to purchase your property under auction during the period when the sheriff plans your foreclosure and entire eviction process. If money is arranged prior to the auction you can buy it, but do not pay an amount which costs you more than the property. Buy a new one!

Conclusion

Foreclosures are painful for the owners of property. There are times in life when hardships fall on us and losing property as a result of it is saddening. Life can never be foreseen but contingencies are inevitable. It is thus recommended to save for the hard times. Foreclosure is a just another loss and can be avoided if life is well planned and money is intelligently spend!

STAGING YOUR HOME FOR A FAST SALE!

Introduction

Some homes sit on the market for days, some for weeks, and some for several months or even years in a worst case scenario. If you're like most homeowners, you're hoping that you'll land a contract quickly.

There is a way that you can make that happen so that your home moves off the market fast. It might surprise you to know that this strategy really doesn't involve a total renovation, either.

You can sell your home fast by staging it. Some people aren't aware of how their home appears to others because they have a sentimental value woven into the mix when they think about the value of their home. Staging helps you see through your prospect's eyes.

How Staging Can Make or Break Your Home Selling Success

There are people who are prepared to sell their home and it shows. These are people who have put the home's best impression center stage. When prospective buyers walk into the house, they can imagine themselves living there.

Homeowners who don't stage their home often look at their house through their own eyes rather than the eyes of a buyer. They think that because they love the home, a buyer will, too - even with any quirky issues or crowded rooms.

They believe that others can look past the lived in atmosphere to see the true gem underneath it all. It doesn't work that way. If a buyer is turned off by what he or she sees when they walk into your house, they don't look past that to see what the home could be like if they lived in it.

What they see is a homeowner who didn't care enough to make the house as presentable as possible. When you stage a home, it makes it look inviting. Potential buyers walk into the house and they're immediately comfortable.

The home looks like it would fit them rather than you. They look around the room that's obviously been well prepared to show its best features and they don't see your sofa in that space.

They picture theirs and how great it would look in the room when they invite guests over or host a family holiday. They feel like the home is one that's been loved and taken care of - and this is what you want them to feel.

Buyers won't balk at paying more to get your house if they feel like it's been well taken care of, but if it looks too well worn, they might question its upkeep. When a buyer goes through a house that hasn't been taken care of and isn't presented nicely on the inside, they start deducting zeroes from your asking price.

Staging your home can help you enjoy faster selling success because a home that's been staged to look its best can come out on top among all the other homes that are listed in your area.

Not only can staging a home for a buyer make it more appealing, but when an appraiser comes to your home, he can clearly see that the home has been taken care of, too.

Though he'll check thoroughly, your home will make a good first impression. And that can lead the appraiser to mark your home's value higher than he might naturally if the home looked too worn.

Focus on Rooms Where Staging Makes the Biggest Difference

Not every single room in your home needs to be staged. They need to be clean and well-presented, but there are some rooms in the home that don't make or break a sale.

For example, while you want a nice looking laundry room, that one doesn't carry the same selling power that other rooms do. You want to start with the entrance to your house.

Your foyer area is a buyer's first introduction to the inside of your home. Unfortunately, it's also the space where most homeowners drop everything off. Keys get tossed onto a small table, shoes get discarded here, school bookbags are left lying around and coats and umbrellas hang from the coat rack or are strewn on a bench.

While for you that's just part of everyday life, for a buyer it looks unkempt like you couldn't even be bothered to straighten up. The kitchen is an area that must be staged well because it's one of the rooms in the house that's a huge selling point.

If your kitchen doesn't look it's best, it can make or break the deal pretty quickly. Your home can be old, but your kitchen can't look like it. If your kitchen looks like it's stuck in the 1970s, what potential buyers are going to see is a whole bunch of expensive renovation work.

Even if you can't afford to renovate your kitchen before you put your house on the market, you can afford to spruce it up with strategic staging. It doesn't cost much to paint cabinets and add some molding.

It also doesn't cost much to put in new curtains or new window blinds. You can also update the hardware on your cabinets. If you have old appliances and can't afford to buy new ones, you can use enamel paint to make them look good.

Each one of your bathrooms should be as inviting as possible. You want to have a great looking tub, shower and countertops. If you have countertops in your bathrooms that have seen better days, you can replace the countertops and it really doesn't cost that much - but the value it will add by helping your home sell is priceless.

Your living room should not look lived in. It should look like a blank canvas that someone else can draw his or her life on. Use all neutral colors and furnishings. Leave the curtains open because it makes the room look bigger.

Have plants and colorful accents in the living room. Group your furniture around a focal point rather than having your sofa, chairs or loveseats flush against walls just to create more space.

To stage the bedrooms for a quick sale, get rid of bulky furniture by stashing it with a friend or in a storage unit. You want the room to look sparse, but not devoid of character.

Having a lot of furniture makes a bedroom look cramped. The bed should be one of the focal points. Cover it with new linen such as white blankets and sheets. Use throw pillows that are colorful and draw out the color from other decorations.

The bed should be a great looking bed even if it's not a very comfortable one. For example, if the bed is too low to the floor, it can make the bedroom look off balance. Settle the bed on risers temporarily to make it look taller and fuller. Remove anything you might normally store under it if it can be seen when a prospective buyer is viewing the room.

Closets are the one thing that many homeowners don't really think about because they don't think the buyer will check. They do. They want to know how much storage space they're going to have.

This isn't a situation like when you have guests in your home. Every space is fair game for taking a look at. Your closet should be neat and well organized, but not filled to the brim with your clothes or other items.

Your dining room should have a great looking table - even if you need to rent one until the home sells. This table should have placemats and be set with nice dishes - and both should be colorful.

Simply adding a bright accent rug beneath a table can help this room look inviting. Make sure there's great lighting and replace any outdated light fixtures. Keep any wall decorations simple here so that the focus can be on the table and the room itself.

The garage is what often makes or breaks a sale when it comes to male buyers. They want a garage that they can picture themselves in. You don't want your garage to look like you're a hoarder.

Clean it out and paint it if needed. Put up hanging hooks to get items off the floor so it looks spacious in the garage. Organize everything and update the lights. Make sure the garage door opens and closes without squeaking or groaning. Clean stains off the floor and make sure there aren't cobwebs everywhere.

Start with a Deep Decluttering Process

To get your home staged for a fast sale, you need to start by deeply decluttering the rooms. When you declutter a home, you make it look bigger like it has more living space, which is something that appeals to potential buyers.

It also prepares you for the letting go and moving on process and lets you show off your home. Most people use some rooms in their homes for things they weren't intended to use the room for - and that can make a house look cramped to a buyer.

For example, sometimes people put workout machines in their living room. This not only looks cluttered, but it immediately gives the buyer the impression that the home is too small.

Start with the foyer. Since this is usually your "drop everything off" area, it will look cluttered and junky. Take out everything except a small table and a nice decorative bowl or flowers.

It will immediately give the impression of openness. In your kitchen, you need to go through your cabinets. Every kitchen has those extra storage container lids floating around that fall out when cabinets are opened.

Pare down all your containers, dishes and utensils and keep the minimum. Your cupboards need to be neat and not piled up haphazardly with dishes or food items.

The same with your pantry. Don't have a half dozen boxes of half-empty cereal and scattered bags of bread lying around. It will make the kitchen look crowded and unclean.

Use baskets or other storage containers to keep things neat. Take the magnets, drawings and anything else off the front and sides of the refrigerator. Put away the family scheduling calendar.

Take the countertop appliances off and put them out of sight. Appliances take up space and make countertops look a lot smaller than they are. Clean off the top of the refrigerator if you store things there.

If you have a lot of knick-knacks, pack them away. Don't leave potholders or any dishwashing detergent or scrubbers out, either. In the bathroom, clear the countertops of anything that you use.

No one wants to see razors, toothpaste or any other toiletry on display. Do the same thing with your shower area. Put away anything that says someone lives in the house.

It makes buyers uncomfortable even though it's an obvious fact. Put away your scale, trashcan and toilet cleaning brush. Don't have bath mats out, either. Make sure everything is sparkling clean.

Clean out drawers, closets and cabinets in the bathroom. Some buyers will take a peek. For the living room, organize any clutter. Put away gaming controllers, TV remotes, magazines and books.

If you have tons of pillows and throw blankets, minimalize it. Take out any toys or baby items like swings or walkers. If you have numerous rugs, take them out because rugs can make a floor space look smaller.

Clear away the clutter from side tables, fireplace mantels and bookshelves. If you have a lot of decorations on the walls, take some of them down. In the bedrooms, you need to take out things that cramp the space.

Not only does this include heavy or large furniture but it also includes what's in your closets. Get rid of clothes you no longer wear, pack up seasonal cloths and organize all the accessories and shoes.

Too many pillows and blankets on a bed can make it look cluttered. Pare down the bedding to make the space look less full. Opting for a minimalist look in the bedroom can make it seem larger than it really is.

Closets have become like junk drawers. Many homeowners shove things into the closet to deal with "later" but that time often never comes. Go through all the closets in your home and take out stuff that you know you're not going to use within the next few months.

Don't leave a bunch of items cluttered on the floor - especially sports equipment. Your closets should look as sparse as possible, because then a potential buyer is thinking about how much room there is rather than how much there isn't.

A dining room needs to be decluttered because it often acts as the place where the kitchen clutter spills over - especially if you have any shelves, or hutches. Clear everything off and if you have a hutch that holds plates or knick-knacks, either remove most of the items or put the hutch in storage.

Don't leave out decorations, stacks of placemats or things like salt and pepper shakers. Deep decluttering a garage means you need to take out the boxes filled with stuff to donate and organize all the seasonal items like Halloween and Christmas decorations.

Anything that's scattered around needs to be picked up and organized. Stuff for the yard like pruning shears, a weedeater, an edger or lawnmowers should be kept neatly together rather than scattered everywhere.

Start by cleaning out the entire garage because it will be easier to declutter that way. Purge what needs to go - including tools that you have in multiple batches. No one needs five hammers. Then as you put things back, use organization products to help keep everything in its place.

Remove Personalized and Sentimental Items

When you put a home on the market, you want it to look as neutral as possible to give it the best chance of selling quickly. One of the first things that you should do before you put your home up for sale is to go through it and pack away the personalized and sentimental items.

There are those who believe that leaving these items in a home help the buyer get a feel for how lovely it will be to live in the home. But the problem with this is that they have a hard time picturing their own lives because yours is so overwhelmingly present.

You don't want the buyer paying attention to your life. You want him paying attention to the house. Leaving sentimental stuff out can hinder the selling process.

By taking out the photos and other items, you create a clean slate for the potential buyers. Plus, you keep the focus on the house rather than on your life. When buyers see photos, these can often catch their attention.

They focus on pictures and sentimental items and forget to envision themselves living in the home. By de-personalizing the home, you enable the buyer to personalize it mentally.

When a buyer walks through the house, you want him thinking about all the features of the home and imagining himself in the rooms. You don't want him thinking about the pictures of the vacation shots you took or the sports events that you were present at.

It's one thing to live in a home and another to sell it - and the two should not be connected when the home goes on the market. Sentimental knick knacks should be packed away just like the pictures.

You want to make a connection with the buyer about the house, not over your figurine collection. You need to take out any memorabilia that you have as well as anything that you collect.

For example, if you collect snowmen figurines and related décor, then you need to put those away. If you have a college diploma on the wall or anything that's personalized with your first or complete name, take that down. You should also remove any sentimental items that reference religion.

Conduct a Thorough Cleaning of Your Home

Your home needs to have a deep cleaning before you put it on the market because there's a different between everyday clean and selling clean. You can clean it yourself if you have the time, but thoroughly cleaning a home can take you a few days to do it right.

Or, you can hire someone and figure that as part of the cost of selling your home. A professional cleaner usually has more experience with cleaning on a deeper level and doesn't often overlook the things that a homeowner will.

A potential buyer will also catch what you don't pay attention to. You need to make sure all the windows are washed on the inside and that the windowsills are clean.

Clean or replace window blinds. Wash all the light globes and fixtures. Wipe down the light switches and wall socket plates. Ceiling fans should be cleaned both at the base, on the blades and the lights.

Remove any cobwebs from the ceilings. Wipe off the tops of the door frames and all the baseboards. Clean beneath all the furniture. If you have rugs, those need to be washed or steam cleaned.

Vacuum under and between couch cushions and other furniture. Wipe down table legs and kitchen chairs. Wash the doorknobs and check and wash areas of the walls that need to be washed.

Sometimes, you may end up having to repaint a room if the paint doesn't look its best. Wash and clean out all the trashcans. Wash off the lights on the porch of your home and make sure the front door and screen door are clean.

Clean out all the cabinets in the house. Wash all the appliances down and clean out the refrigerator and freezer. Make sure the disposal is clean and smells good. Make sure that all the towel racks are dusted.

Remove any discoloration in the bathrooms and clean the mirrors. Put fresh sheets and blankets on the bed. Organize everything. Sweep, vacuum and mop the floors as needed.

If you have carpeting, steam clean it or get it professionally cleaned to remove odors. Wash all the pet bedding - and the pets! Clean all their toys and dishes.

Use air fresheners or scented candles in the rooms, but not anything overpowering.

You can become immune to the scents in your home - like pet odors - so ask someone to come over and tell you if the house has a strange or unpleasant odor.

Make a Decision on What to Repair or Remodel

Few homes are in such great shape that they can go on the market without needing some repairs and remodeling. Bumps and accidents happen and these can result in dings or holes in the drywall.

Sometimes a ceiling will develop a cosmetic crack that doesn't impact the integrity of the ceiling. You'll want to repair any drywall damage so that the walls of the home are in good shape.

If you have an appliance that's not working, whether or not you fix that is up to you - but keep in mind that a good portion of buyers want to add a contingency for the appliances to be included in the sale.

If your heating and air conditioning unit isn't working correctly, pay to have that repaired before you try to sell it because this can cost you a sale. Anything that's a big ticket item such as a heating and air unit is something that buyers don't want to have to deal with.

If your sinks or tubs have leaky faucets, fix those. Look at the flooring in all the rooms in your house. If it looks dirty, clean it - if it's torn, then you need to repair it.

Any window frames that show any wood damage should be fixed as well as any windows in the home that might be cracked. Fix any areas of the home where there's been water damage.
If you know for certain that something in your home might not pass inspection because it's not up to code, bring it up to code. If the roof has some trouble spots, fix those - but it could be that your home needs a new roof.

You don't necessarily have to put on a new roof, but if it's clear the home needs one because the current one is old or has been repaired, then you can negotiate replacing it as part of the sale.

Just know that this usually results in calculations in the buyer's favor. A buyer will usually ask for things to be repaired. Some of them, you'll want to give on, but others, you might not want to.

If it's cosmetic, let that be the buyer's responsibility. This might include something like taking care of painting the walls a new color or replacing doorknobs they don't like or changing the landscaping.

Other repairs or fixes, you'll want to give on. If the roof is going to cost $8,000 to replace, then you may want to pay to have it done yourself, because you'll pay more if you end up negotiating part or all of the cost of replacing it from the selling price of the house.

When it comes to knowing what to remodel, the key is to focus on what helps you sell the home. This means the kitchen and bathrooms. But there are also other repairs and renovations that can help your house sell quickly.

Insulating the attic is one of them. Adding a deck or a patio is another. Putting on new siding and windows is also a good remodeling project to boost profits in the sale. Little renovations, such as replacing the front door and the gutters, can pay you back in profits.

Add Props to Make Your Home Feel Inviting

While you might be selling a house, buyers are looking for a place that they can call home. By setting your home up so that it looks inviting, you can give someone the desire that this is the place they want to be.

If you have a lot of books, it can make a home look cluttered, but a couple of old hardback books, especially the classics, can be used as a prop on a coffee table or end table.

One home prop that you'll often see suggested is having a bowl of fruit out - such as apples. But the problem with apples as a prop is twofold. First, it's been done so often that they tend to kind of fade into the background.

Second, if you forget to keep an eye on them and the apples start to turn mushy, it can fill the space with an unpleasant odor. Instead of apples in a decorative bowl, use lemons.

Not only do you get a bright pop of color that reminds people of sunny days, but lemons can outlast apples and they look great in any room. One way to add props to a bathroom that helps it look more inviting is to check out what a spa experience offers.

Then put props in your bathroom that make potential buyers think of luxury and relaxation. You can start by adding plush towels. You can go with whatever color you'd like, but keep in mind that thick, white towels make people think of spas.

Set up a bathtub tray with candles and serenity rocks. Throughout the home, use scented candles as props that remind people of warmth - such as vanilla, red apples or mild cinnamon.

Use accent pillows - and if you're not sure what color, look at the wall art in the room for inspiration to draw from. Pillows make a home look inviting as well as luxurious.

Pre-Tour Your Home Through the Lens of Your Senses

By now, you've reached the stage where you're just about ready to put the home on the market. You think you have everything that can possible be done taken care of and the home is as appealing as it can be.

To make sure that your home really is market-ready, you're going to want to do your own tour through the rooms to make sure you haven't missed anything. The best way to do this is by walking through the home while paying attention to your senses.

It might even be helpful to take a small notepad with you and write down your first impression of the room as it pertains to each of your senses. When you walk into a room, write down the first scent that you notice.

It could be that in the bedroom, the first thing you can smell is the fabric softener that you used on the linens or on your clothes. You want the scent to be fresh and appealing.

Some fabric softeners have a good, but common scent. You want the room to smell inviting rather than like your laundry. In the kitchen, breathe deeply to see if you can pick up on any scents from the trashcan or from the garbage disposal.

Go through the rooms and listen for what you hear. If there's anything distracting, like a loud clock ticking, you may want to take that down. If you walk across the floor and it squeaks, investigate if that's something that you need to take care of.

When you push open a door, pay attention to the sound that it makes. The way a room looks makes a lasting impression on a buyer - so when you pre-tour your home, see if it looks serene and welcoming. Look for anything that's out of place or captures attention in a bad way.

Head Outside and Spiff Up Your Curb Appeal

What's outside the home is going to be the first thing that tells a buyer if he wants to see the home. Curb appeal is something that can set your home up to sell fast - and it doesn't have to cost a whole lot to give a home this kind of help.

You want to make sure the lawn looks good and that it's edged. For instant curb appeal, have flowers in a flower bed or in decorative pots or use greenery. Put flowers around the trees instead of mulch.

Paint the shutters and the front door. Put in new hardware on the door or paint it. Upgrade the porch light. Paint or buy new house numbers and renovate or replace the mailbox.

If you have a concrete entryway, clean or stain the concrete to make it look like tiles. Add hanging plants. Ferns are always popular as are colorful flowers. Put up veneer panels to cover the concrete foundation of your house. Install a heating and air conditioning screen to camouflage the unit.

Use the Staging Results to Take Pictures for Your Promos

Once you have your home staged, you're going to want to have professional photos taken. This will range in price and some can be expensive - but what you pay out in good quality photos, you will reap by having your home sell quickly.

If you don't want to hire a professional photographer or it's just not in the budget, then you can do it yourself with a little bit of research. You need to look up tutorials for the best angles to use when taking a picture.

Keep in mind that this angle won't always be the same in a different room. When the home is completely ready to put on the market and you have the inside and outside of it staged, then you want to make sure you photograph it at the best time.

Use natural sunlight and make sure the curtains and blinds are open. Take pictures of the room from different sides to make sure you get all the best features.

You'll want to take plenty of photographs - but you won't use them all. Make sure you get low, eye-level shots. These kinds of shots look better in flat media like ads rather than high shots.

Don't tilt the camera up, down or sideways. Keep it straight. Make sure you balance the photograph. If you take a shot of the exterior of your home, you don't want the house way off to the left or the right.

Use your normal focus inside and out, and don't zoom in. Don't try to take pictures on days when the weather is bad. Your house just won't photograph well.

If you have a home with a lot of windows that let in natural light, you can play up this feature, but try photographing your home from the outside just as night is almost there, too.

Have all the lights on shining from the inside out and it will create a beautiful photo with the lights at a soft glow like the house is waiting to welcome in the buyer.

RENTING HOUSE OR APARTMENTS

Apartment Hunting Tips

Apartment hunting can be very daunting for some potential renters. Often the variety of options available to these renters is a source of overwhelming frustration for the renters. With so many appealing options it can be difficult to choose just one. However, there are some tips which can help to ease the process of apartment hunting. The process of finding the perfect apartment can be broken down into three simple steps. The first step is to set a budget. Next the renter should research their available options and then comparison shop to determine which option is the best.

Set a Budget First

For many renters the most important consideration is how much they are willing to spend on an apartment per month. For this reason it should come as no surprise that the first step in the apartment hunting process should include establishing a budget. Renters should consider their monthly income and subtract out all of their monthly expenses from this amount. Monthly expenses should include all bills which are paid regularly as well as money spent on food, entertainment and miscellaneous items each month. The renter may also wish to subtract out an additional amount to allow for some savings each month as well as emergencies. The total left after these subtractions is the amount the renter is able to spend on an apartment per month. Once this amount is established the renter will have a better understanding of the type of apartment they are able to afford.

Research Available Properties

Once a budget has been established, the renter should begin researching the properties which fall within his budget range. It is likely to consider properties which are slightly above the range as well as properties which are slightly below the range. Doing this will allow the renter to see if there is an opportunity to either make improvements on the amount of monthly spending to allow for the renting of a more expensive property. The renter can also determine whether or not they feel there is the opportunity to negotiate a lower rental rate on a particular property.

When initially researching properties, the renter does not necessarily have to visit each property. Most of the pricing information can be obtained from resources such as Internet websites, newspapers and rental magazines. Since pricing is the primary concern at this point, the initial research will enable the renter to eliminate properties which are too far out of their price range.

Comparison Shop

Once the renter has narrowed down his list of possible apartment complexes to a more manageable number it is time to start visiting these properties. It is during this step that the renter will really get a feel for the quality of the apartment as well as the amount and quality of amenities offered by the complex. This is very important because this information can be used to decide between properties which are otherwise very similar.

The comparison shopping process is also worthwhile because it gives the renter some bargaining power in negotiating more favorable rent rates. Renters who have visited a number of apartments likely have a good idea of the going rate in a particular area for a particular size apartment. These renters can use this information to potentially convince some leasing agents to lower their prices at least a little bit. There will not likely be huge drops in price from these negotiations but it will likely be enough to be considered worthwhile.

Before Renting an Apartment

Renting an apartment is a very serious decision which warrants a great deal of attention before a final decision is made. When choosing an apartment to rent, renters have a variety of factors to consider including, but not limited to, price, size, location, amenities, whether or not they want a roommate and how long they want to stay in the apartment. Those who plan to rent an apartment should consider all of their options before making a decision to ensure they are making the best possible decision. This article will discuss the importance of considering all of the possible options as well as the possibility of having roommates and the importance of reading contracts carefully.

Consider All of the Possible Options

When renting an apartment, the renter should first investigate all of the options available to him to ensure he is able to make an informed decision. This is important because the renter may not even be aware of all of the available options until he starts to for an apartment. The best way to find out what type of apartments are available is to do some research on the Internet and in newspapers and rental magazines and then start visiting apartments which seem interesting. In visiting the apartments the renter will get a better idea of the size and types of amenities which are available in his price range. He will also begin to learn more about the types of amenities available. This is important because not all apartments will offer the same amenities. Renters may not find what they are looking for unless they visit a few places before making a decision.

Consider the Possibility of Roommates

Deciding whether or not to have a roommate or multiple roommates is one of the important decisions a renter will have to make. This is an important decision because roommates can make a living situation either significantly better or significantly worse depending on a number of factors. These factors may include compatibility of the roommates, ability to pay the rent and ability to assist in the household activities.

Having roommates can make an apartment more affordable. Often larger apartments may be more affordable for two people than a smaller apartment would be for one renter. Additionally, apartments designed for two or more people often have a larger overall living space with a larger kitchen, dining room and family room. This makes the possibility of roommates very appealing to some renters.

However, there are some caveats to making the decision to live with a roommate. Care should be taken to carefully screen potential roommates to ensure they are not potentially harmful. Strangers do not present the only potential roommate problems. Problems may even occur when the roommate is a trusted friend. In these cases, compatible living styles may be the issue. For example, if one roommate likes to stay up late and listen to music or watch television and the other roommate likes to go to sleep early there can be some conflicts if compromises are not made. Also, if one of the roommates is particularly neat and the other rather messy, conflicts may arise.

Read the Contract Carefully

Whether a renter opts to have a roommate or not and regardless of the type of apartment they select, the renter should be careful to read the contract before signing it. This is important because a rental agreement is a legal document and the renter should understand this document before they sign the agreement. Many renters may never need to know the exact information in their contract document but if a dispute arises, the renter should be aware of his rights. Additionally, the renter should pay special attention to any sections of the contract which specify the landlordís ability to evict the tenant. Contract sections specifying the requirements of the renter are also very important. This may include requirements for breaking the lease agreement in the event that the renter has to move before the lease period ends.

Benefits of Renting

While there are some renters who view renting an apartment or a house as a failure, there are others who see the benefits there are to be gained from renting a property as opposed to purchasing a property. Some of the benefits of renting include the ability to save money while renting for the purpose of purchasing a home, few maintenance requirements and the inclusion of amenities which the renter would not likely be able to afford if they were to purchase a home instead of renting. Although there are some negative aspects to renting an apartment, this article will focus exclusively on the benefits of renting a property.

The Ability to Save Money

Being able to save up a great deal of money for the purpose of making a down payment on a dream home is just one of the many great advantages to renting a property. Many homeowners were able to realize their dream of homeownership only after living in a rental property for a certain amount of time. Although renting is often criticized as throwing money away because it does not result in equity, the ability to save money while renting is unparalleled

Rent for an apartment is usually considerably less expensive than the monthly mortgage on a home. The home is also typically much bigger than the rental property but in cases where the renter is renting for the sole purpose of saving money, the value of renting cannot be denied. Depending on how long the renter stays in the apartment, they may save hundreds or even thousands of dollars during the course of the rental agreement.

No Maintenance Properties

Another advantage to renting a property is there is typically little or no maintenance required by the renter. This is especially true in an apartment situation. The renter may be responsible for small items such as changing light bulbs but more extensive repairs such as leaks in plumbing or clogs in drains are typically handled by the maintenance staff of the rental property.

Additionally common areas such as grassy areas or gardens are maintained by the maintenance staff. The exception is usually when the renter rents a home as opposed to the apartment. In these cases the renter may still not be responsible for small repairs but might be obligated to take care of items such as maintaining the grass.

Worthwhile Amenities

Another advantage to apartment living is often the amenities offered to residence. Such amenities might include usage of the pool, an exercise room, meeting spaces and a theater room. In most cases these amenities are offered free of charge to resident and their guests. Many renters who might be able to purchase a home would not likely be able to purchase a home with amenities such as a pool, fully equipped exercise room and a home theater.

These items are often considered luxurious and are not available in the majority of homes which are on the market at any particular time. In fact searching for homes which specifically have these features may severely limit the number of search results and may result in no search results at all when these features are searched in conjunction with a typical price range. However, those who rent can enjoy access to these amenities. They may pay more in rent than those in a comparable apartment complex without these amenities but they are also still likely saving a considerable amount of money each month as long as they are budgeting wisely and have chosen a rental property within their price range.

Breaking a Lease on a Rental Agreement

Most rental agreements have a section regarding the renter breaking the lease agreement. While there is also likely a section or several sections regarding when the leasing agent can evict the renter, the section on breaking the lease should be of particular interest to those who might be in a position to have to break the lease some day. Renters should understand these contract terms so they can make an informed decision. Additionally the renter should consider all costs associated with breaking the lease. This includes both financial costs as well as emotional costs.

Understand the Contract Terms

Renters should review their rental agreement carefully before signing this document. The rental agreement is a legally binding document which should be given proper consideration before entering into the agreement. This is important because understanding these terms will be essential if the need to break the lease becomes a reality.

Rental agreements typically do allow the renter to break the lease but not without some form of penalty. This penalty usually comes in the form of requiring the renter to give a specified amount of notice before the contract is up and also requires the renter to pay a sum of money to break the rental agreement. A notice of 30 days and a lease break amount equal to one monthís rent are common penalties associated with breaking a lease, however, individual leasing agents may impose penalties which are either harsher or less severe.

Consider the Costs of Breaking the Lease

As previously mentioned there is typically a fee associated with breaking a lease. This fee is often set equal to one month's rent. While paying this fee may seem excessive there are some instances in which it is an economically good decision to break the contract even though there is a financial penalty imposed.

Consider the example of a homeowner who is the process or relocating due to a job change. The homeowner may opt to rent an apartment in the new state while the house is put up for sale in the previous state. If the renter enters into a 12 month contract under the supposition that it will take this long to sell the old house and purchase a new house, he may be surprised if his other house sells quickly and he finds a home in his new state rather quickly. This may all occur within a matter of 2-3 months.

The renter has the option to stay in the apartment until the rental agreement nears expiration and then start looking for a home. However, this option runs the risk that the home he previously found will not likely be available. The renters other option is to place a bid on the new house and plan on breaking the lease if he is able to close on the new house. In this case, the renter would be saddled with both a rent and a mortgage for 9-10 months.

This will likely be significantly more expensive than the price the renter would pay to break the lease.

Breaking the Lease is Not Always a Financial Decision

The decision to break a lease is not always completely a financial decision. There are sometimes emotional components which factor into the equation. For example a renter may have only 1-2 months remaining on his rental agreement when he is offered a dream job which will require him to relocate immediately. Although breaking the lease that late in the agreement is usually not financially wise, the renter may make this decision to avoid missing out on a dream job.

Caring For a Rental Property

Those who live in a rental property may have questions regarding how they should care for their domicile. While treating the property with respect and not intentionally doing damage to the property should be understood there are other gray areas where renters may not be sure what their rights and responsibilities are in the rental situation. In most of these cases, these questions can be resolved by carefully reviewing the rental agreement. This can provide the renter a great deal of insight regarding which items will be corrected by the leasing agent and which items are the responsibilities of the renter.

Treat the Property Like it Is Your Home

The heading to this subsection is certainly appropriate in theory but in reality it may not be true. The theory behind treating a rental property like it is your home is that you should treat the rental property in the same way you would treat your own home. This means the renter should not intentionally damage or otherwise neglect the rental property. It also implies that the renter should care for the rental property by making necessary repairs as they arise.

However, the reality of this heading is not true because renters are often not free to treat a rental property like it was their home. Homeowners are free to make modifications at any time to their property. Renters do not have this option and are only allowed to make modifications which are permitted by the contract agreement. These permissible modifications are usually rather insignificant in nature.

Seek Assistance from the Property Manager When Warranted

Renters should also seek assistance from the property manager when there are repairs which fall under the jurisdiction of the property owner or manager. Such repairs might include items such as unclogging drains, fixing appliances and making modifications to the residence such as installing lighting features. Although the renter may be capable of performing some or all of these actions, the rental agreement may specify these items are the responsibility of the property owner or manager. Renters who attempt to fix these items may be held liable for damages which occur during these attempts.

Similarly, the rental agreement may imply, by omission, that certain items are the responsibility of the renter. These may be small items such as changing light bulbs or similar items. In these cases the renter is free to make the adjustments. However, in other situations where the rental agreement specifies the apartment manager will handle certain complaints, these complaints should be called to the attention of management.

When the Property Manager Isnít Doing His Job

Renters may encounter a problem where the apartment manager is not being responsive to his complaints and is not addressing situations which are brought to his attention. When this occurs the renter may have no choice but to bring this to the attention of the property managerís supervisor. When a property manager is required to make certain repairs and address certain issues and fails to do so, he is creating a hazard for the members of the community. This is why the renter should not allow these transgressions to occur. The renter should also not be fearful of retaliation by the property manager because the contract will likely specify the renter's rights to complain to a higher authority about the quality of service they are receiving.

Consider the Amenities

The amenities on a rental property can often be the deciding factor for many renters. The available amenities may make a less affordable property seem more appealing. Conversely a property which is more expensive may be considered worthwhile if the amenities offered are considered valuable enough to compensate for the higher price. When making this decision, homeowners should consider their own personal preferences as well as their budgetary constraints to make an informed decision. Before making a decision to rent a property, the renter should carefully consider which amenities are necessary, which amenities are optional but highly desired and how much the renter is willing to pay for these amenities.

What Amenities Do You Really Need?

Although many of the amenities offered by rental properties are not exactly necessary to live, there are some amenities which some renters would not consider renting a property without. An exercise room is one such example. While this is certainly not necessary, many renters prefer having this option. Without an onsite exercise facility, many renters would have to consider joining a gym for their exercise needs. This will likely increase the monthly expenses significantly and, depending on the location, may also make it inconvenient for the renter to visit the gym. An onsite exercise is significantly more convenient than traveling to a gym in another location. For this reason many renters consider the added expense associated with an onsite exercise facility to be worthwhile.

Some renters may even consider only renting an apartment in a facility that has a pool. Although this is not a necessity some renters, especially in warm climates, might only consider living in a rental property where there is access to a pool especially if the majority of rental properties include this amenity.

What Amenities Do You Really Want?

In addition to the amenities a renter feels he needs, there are some amenities which may be desired as opposed to necessary. A movie theater may be an example of this type of amenity. Renters may not decide against a rental property which does not have this feature but may be more inclined to select a property that has this feature as opposed to one that does not as long as the price is comparable.

A meeting space may be another example of an amenity which may not be required but that many renters are willing to pay extra to have. Renters who entertain frequently may enjoy this type of amenity because it affords them extra space for entertaining. They may be able to easily invite eight or more people over for a dinner party if there is meeting space available but this might not be possible if the renter were confined to their apartment.

Are You Paying Too Much for Amenities?

While some amenities may be viewed as necessary and others may merely be viewed as worthwhile and still others may be viewed as superfluous, the most important decision renters will have to make is how much they are willing to pay for these amenities. Comparison shopping may be the best way to determine whether or not certain amenities are financially worthwhile.

Renters who are considering apartments of similar size in the same geographic region should consider the amenities offered as well as the price of the apartment. Apartments of similar size in the same area should be fairly close in price. However, an apartment which offers more advanced amenities might be significantly higher in price. Renters should list the available amenities and use this information in making cost comparisons. This information can be used to determine whether or not the renter is willing to pay a higher price for such amenities. Renters who conclude the additional cost is not warranted have determined that the prices of the amenities are not worthwhile to them and they are likely to choose the more affordable apartment which features fewer amenities.

Dealing with Neighbors in an Apartment

One of the major disadvantages to renting an apartment is the potential for conflict with the neighbors. While some renters may foster incredible relationships with all of their neighbors and never once have a disagreement with a neighbor this is not a likely scenario. Most renters experience at least one instance of dissatisfaction with their neighbors. They may or may not confront the neighbor about this issue but it is likely to cause at least some tension in the living situation. In some cases avoiding the issue can cause the problem to worsen. In other situations, discussing the issue can make the situation worse.

Paper Thin Walls

Although most modern apartment buildings are built with a fair amount of insulation, there is still the real possibility of neighbors in an apartment building hearing music, television, conversation or other noises emanating from a neighborís apartment on a regular basis. This is due to the close proximity of the apartments to each other as well as the common practice of having at least one shared wall among neighbors in an apartment complex. Renters should be aware of this and make an effort to avoid noises which will likely be heard through the walls during nights or early in the morning when others are likely to be sleeping.

Being Considerate of Others

Consideration for others is one of the key elements which can make apartment living more bearable and less prone to conflict. For example, while renters are free to listen to music in their own apartment, they should limit listening to music at a loud decibel to daylight hours when it is not likely that other residents are trying to sleep.

Residents in an apartment complex should also be conscientious when throwing parties. This is important because the renter is responsible for the actions of his guests. Therefore the renter should ensure his guests are not causing discomfort for residents of the apartment complex.

When Your Schedule is Unusual

Finally renters who have an unusual schedule may have a great deal of difficulty functioning in an apartment complex. This includes, but is not limited to, renters who work a night shift and sleep during the day. The unusual schedule kept by these renters makes them more prone to being disturbed by other renters who assume everyone residing in the complex sleeps at roughly the same time.

Unfortunately renters in this situation may have to make an effort to make their living situation bearable. While discussing the situation with the neighbors is certainly worthwhile, it is unrealistic to expect the neighbors to remain exceedingly quite during the daytime hours. Many residents do chores such as vacuuming during this time which can resonate in the apartment of another renter. However, asking the neighbor to do these types of activities in the evening is not feasible because the neighbor would likely be disturbing a number of other neighbors by doing so.

This is why the renter with the unusual schedule is often required to make changes to make the living situation workable. This may include purchasing and using earplugs while sleeping or investing in a white noise machine which can help to drowned out ambient noise and make the environment more conducive to sleeping. Additionally, the renter with the unusual schedule should make an effort to be quite during hours in which they are awake but the majority of neighbors are likely sleeping.

Decorating a Rental Apartment

Those who live in a rental apartment are usually quite limited in the amount of decorating they are able to do. This can have the impact of making a rental apartment not quite feel like a real home. In many cases the rental apartment is painted a bright white and residents often feel as though this color is somewhat impersonal but are not able to repaint the walls to a more appealing color. This is just one example of the decorating restrictions which may be placed on an individual renting an apartment. There may be other restrictions and reading the contract carefully will help the renter to determine what is allowed and what is not allowed.

Review the Contract Carefully

Renters who are living in an apartment should review their contract documents carefully before they begin decorating their apartment. This is important because there may be some common decorating items such as painting or installation of shelving which may not be allowed by the contract documents. Decorating in any manner which is strictly prohibited may result in harsh penalties. These penalties might involve the assessment of fees at the conclusion of the rental period or possibly even eviction.

Most standard decorating items such as hanging pictures are usually acceptable but some particularly strict policies may either prohibit this completely or place restrictions on the type of nails which may be used or the methods of patching the holes. Renters who have questions regarding whether or not specific decorating actions are permissible or prohibited should contact their leasing agent before taking action. This will help to ensure the renter is not penalized in the future for their actions.

Additionally, if the leasing agent tells the renter it is acceptable to perform an action prohibited by the rental agreement, the renter should always ask for a signed, written document stating the exception to the contract. This is helpful because the leasing agent may not remember making an exception to the rule or may not even still be working at the property when the renterís lease expires.

Consider Whether or Not Modifications are Reversible

When renters in an apartment living situation are making decorating decisions, one of the most important factors to consider is whether or not a modification to the apartment is reversible. In most cases, the action is likely to be permissible as long as it is easily reversible.

However, the case of painting the apartment is a common exception to this rule. Although painting can easily be reversed, most apartment complexes due not allow residents to pain the apartment in which they reside. This is because although painting is often reversible, the process of returning the wall to the original color is not always easy.

Irreversible modifications such as removing walls or adding permanent fixtures to the apartment are typically not considered acceptable when decorating a rental apartment. Although even major modifications are typically not completely irreversible, most leasing agents would consider modifications which require the assistance of a general contract to be permanent in nature. Conversely, small modifications such as nail holes to hang pictures are considered reversible because they can easily be corrected. Again, if the renter is unsure of whether or not an action is permissible, they should seek clarification from the leasing agent.

Consider the Security Deposit

Most renters pay a security deposit before they take possession of the apartment. This security deposit is collected to protect against damages which may be caused by the renter during the course of the rental agreement. The leasing agent may expect to need to do some minor cleaning or a few small repairs after the renter vacates the premises. However, a deposit large enough to cover the cost of more significant repairs is often collected to provide the leasing agent with some protection in case the renter damages the apartment and leaves it in need of considerable repair.

Decorating a Rental House

Those who opt to rent a house as opposed to an apartment may still be held to certain restrictions regarding the type of decorating which can be done on the property. These restrictions may be stricter or more lenient than those typically enforced when a renter is renting an apartment property. This will largely depend on the preferences of the homeowners. Homeowners who do not want to see major modifications done to the property may place strict restrictions while those who want to see the property improved may allow the renter a great deal of freedom in their decorating options.

How Much is Too Much?

This can be a difficult question to answer when used in reference to how much decorating is permissible in a rental house. Many renters opt for a situation where they are renting a house as opposed to an apartment strictly because they are looking for more freedom in their decorating options. However, the renter may find this desired freedom is not available to them.

Some homeowners may allow the renter to make minor decorating changes such as painting the walls, hanging up pictures or installing decorative shelving. However, more extensive decorating items such as new flooring, knocking down walls or putting in windows might not be considered acceptable by some homeowners while others may allow the renter to perform such actions. Still others may require this type of work to be done but may place restrictions which specify all improvement work shall be done by a qualified professional.

Check with the Homeowner

When considering doing some decorating in a rental house, the renter should first carefully review all of their contract documents. This is important because the contract may clearly prohibit certain items. In this case the renter would know for sure that they are not allowed to perform these actions. However, the renter should not count on the contract documents to spell out every possible scenario. Therefore if a renter is considering making modifications to the rental house they should consult the owner before performing any work. They should also ask the homeowner to provide a written statement expressing their approval of the work to be completed.

The homeowner is the renters best resource of these types of questions because the homeowner has the best understanding of their intentions when they wrote the rental contract. They might have specified that no renter can alter the appearance of the apartment without the consent of the homeowner but they may have meant for this statement to only apply to certain situations. In these cases, seeking clarification and written approval can be very beneficial to the renter.

When in Doubt; Leave it Out

If renters are in doubt about whether or not to perform a specific decorating action and are unable to reach the homeowner for clarification, they should opt not to make the changes. This can save the renter a great deal of time and money in the long run by preventing them from incurring excess charges for repair of the apartment and wasting a great deal of time making an improvement which the homeowner may ask to have reversed in a short period of time. This is why renters should assume an action is prohibited unless they have concrete proof otherwise.

Do Not Let the Furnishings Fool You

Renters who are viewing apartment complexes are often led to furnished models which have been tastefully decorated. Although the furnishings in these model apartments are usually very aesthetically appealing they also usually serve another purpose as well. This other purpose is to make the room appear larger than it is. There are decorator and furnishing techniques which can make a room in an apartment appear considerably larger than it really is. The size of the bed, the amount of furniture and the layout of the furniture are all items which should be carefully considered when viewing model apartments. This article will cover these three items and will provide useful information for renters who are trying to evaluate furnished apartments.

The Size of the Bed

Determining the size of the bed in a model apartment is important for the purposes of evaluating the apartment. If you are unsure of the size of the bed used in the model, ask the leasing agent for clarification. This is important because if the bed used in the model is a full size bed and your own bed is a king size bed, it will be difficult to make assumptions about the size of the bedroom. The differences in a full size bed and a queen size bed may not be as noticeable but renters should be aware a queen bed will result in less free space in the room. If the bed used in the model is not the same size as your own bed, take

129

measurements to determine how well your own bed will fit in the room.

Is There Enough Furniture?

When viewing a furnished, model important it is important to note whether or not there is enough furniture in the room. For example there may be a kitchen table and only two chairs instead of four. This may make the room appear larger to those who are viewing the apartment but they are likely going to be disappointed when they move in.

Consider the furniture in other rooms as well. For example a bedroom which only has a bed and a nightstand will be decidedly less crowded than a bedroom which has a bed, two nightstands and a dresser. Your furniture may not be exactly the same size as the model furniture but there should be comparable items in each room.

Does the Layout Make Sense?

Renters should also carefully consider the layout of the furniture when visiting a furnished apartment. An apartment may feature all of the pieces of furniture the renter expects to see in the room but may position these pieces of furniture in a way that is not logical. Consider the family room as an example. There may be a couch, an entertainment center, a television set, a coffee table and two end tables but if these items are positioned strangely it can be deceiving. Most renters arrange their living room furniture in a manner which makes the area conducive to conversations as well as viewing of the television. If the television is positioned where it is not viewable from any of the seating options, the layout of the room is somewhat unnatural. It is not likely to be similar to the layout used by the renter and therefore does not offer an accurate representation of how the space will likely be used.

Finding a Rental Apartment

Those who do not wish to purchase a home may find that renting an apartment is an ideal solution for their situation. An apartment can offer many of the conveniences of home ownership such as a functional living space offering the renter the opportunity to eat, sleep and entertain in their domicile. Renting can also offer additional amenities such as meeting spaces, pools, weight rooms or exercise equipment. These types of amenities are optional and may not be available in all rental situations. This article will discuss the art of finding a rental apartment that will suit all of your needs.

Renters who are interested in finding an apartment should consider a number of factors. These factors might include their budget, location, requirements and desires. The key to finding an ideal apartment to rent is to strike a balance of these factors. For example a renter may desire amenities such as a pool, hot tub, sauna, steam room and onsite theater but these options may not be available in his budget range. In this scenario, the renter will likely have to make some compromises which may include realizing not all of the desired amenities are feasible within the current budget or making the decision to allot additional funds for rent.

Set a Budget First

Budget is one of the primary concerns for those looking to rent an apartment. For these individuals, the search for an apartment should begin with the process of narrowing down the search for apartments to those that are within the set budget. It might be worthwhile to look at a few apartments which are priced slightly above the budget. This is because, depending on the vacancy rate, there may be an opportunity to negotiate a slightly lower rate which can bring the rent of the apartment to within the renterís budgetary constraints. Alternately the renter may decide he is willing to pay a little more for certain features such as a larger living space, more desirable amenities or a choice location.

Choose a Location

Location is a very important factor for renters to consider when searching for an apartment. An ideal location is one which is not to far from family, work or leisure activities. Again this is a matter of personal preference and will depend largely on the desires of the renter. Some renters may favor a shorter commute to work because it affords them more time to spend with their families. Other renters may not have family close by and may opt to rent an apartment further from work if it is near access to an activity they enjoy such as skiing in the mountains or surfing in the ocean.

Renters should also consider the surrounding areas when choosing an apartment. Some renters may enjoy being near social activities such as movie theaters and shopping centers while others may prefer to rent an apartment in an established neighborhood apart from the commercial areas. Likewise some renters may prefer living in an apartment where there is nearby access to public transportation while others may not favor this option.

Consider the Requirements and Amenities

Finally, renters should consider their requirements and preferred amenities when searching for an apartment. Requirements might include criteria such as two or more bedrooms, two or more bathrooms or a minimum square footage. These are criteria which the renter feels they must have in order to function in the apartment. For example a family with two children might need 2-3 bedrooms while a single person may be able to function with only one bedroom. However, a single person who works from home may require an additional bedroom to use as an office.

Renters should also consider the features they would like to have in an apartment complex. This may include access to a pool or exercise equipment, the use of a home theater for residents or meeting facilities which are only available to residents. Renters should carefully consider these options and determine which are most important to them.

Furnished or Unfurnished?

Renters will often be faced with the decision of whether to opt for a furnished apartment or an unfurnished apartment. The majority of apartments available for rent are likely to be unfurnished apartments but there are some apartments which are available with furnishings. There are some situations in which it makes sense to choose a furnished apartment. Likewise there are situations in which a furnished apartment is not a good idea. This article will discuss these situations in an effort to assist the reader in determining whether or not it is better to rent a furnished apartment or an unfurnished apartment.

What Does Furnished Mean?

A furnished apartment may mean different things to different people. Some renters may expect a furnished apartment to have each and every room completely furnished with every possible piece of furniture. Typical furnishings may include a bed, a dresser, nightstands, alarm clock with built in radio, a television, stereo equipment, DVD player, an entertainment center, couch, coffee table, end tables, kitchen table and kitchen chairs. It may also include dining room furniture such as a dining room table, chairs and a curial cabinet. Others may assume a furnished apartment includes only the necessary furnishings such as a bed, couch, kitchen table and chairs. This essentially eliminates all electrical equipment as well as furniture deemed to be decorative in nature such as a coffee table, end tables or nightstands.

When is a Furnished Apartment a Good Idea?

A furnished apartment is a good idea for recent college graduates who lived on campus in a dorm room prior to graduation. These students likely have very little furniture of their own. In this case, renting a furnished apartment may be more economical than purchasing enough furniture to live comfortably in the apartment.

The overall cost of a furnished apartment may be higher in the long run because the renter may pay more but those who are unable to pay a great deal of money upfront to furnish an apartment might not mind paying this additional amount. For these renters, they are not likely to notice the impact of a slightly higher monthly rent payment but they would definitely feel the impact of significant purchases such as a bed, couch or dining room set.

When is an Unfurnished Apartment a Good Idea?

There are certain situations in which an unfurnished apartment is a good idea. This includes a situation where the renter has already accumulated enough furniture to furnish the entire apartment. In this case, selecting a furnished apartment would not make sense because the renter would have to find a location to store either his own furniture or the furniture supplied by the apartment complex. The cost of storage can add up very quickly. Additionally, the renter probably pays a higher rent to stay in a furnished apartment.

An unfurnished apartment is also a good idea when the renter currently does not have any furniture but is looking forward to purchasing furniture and has already saved up enough money to make these purchases. In this situation the renter will likely select an unfurnished apartment and plan on shopping for furniture almost immediately after taking possession of the rental property.

Storing Extra Furniture

Renters who opt for a fully furnished apartment when they already have a sufficient amount of furniture have to determine what they will do with their furniture while they are staying in the rental apartment. The options are basically as follows:

* Sell or give away all currently owned furniture
* Store your own furniture
* Store the furniture which comes with the apartment

While each of the above options is certainly valid, the renter should seriously consider whether or not they want to pay additional storage fees just to rent a furnished apartment. Renters who plan to sell or donate their current furniture do not face this dilemma but those who plan to store one set of furniture should carefully consider the price of storage. They should also consult with the leasing agent to determine if there are any contract items which prohibit placing furniture owned by the apartment complex in an offsite storage facility. There may be provisions which allow for these items to be stored but require them to be stored onsite.

Getting Your Security Deposit Back

For many renters the subject of the security deposit is somewhat of a touchy subject. Most renters assume they should receive their security deposit back in its entirety as long as there is no significant damage done to the apartment. However, this is rarely true as there are number of factors which contribute to whether or not the security deposit or a portion of the deposit will be returned to the renter when they vacate the premises.

Did You Do Any Major Damage?

Certainly doing major damage to the apartment such as putting holes in the walls, breaking appliances or tearing up the flooring may warrant the security deposit being kept but even in these cases the leasing agent must justify these costs. In other words the leasing agent cannot use one damaged item to justify keeping the whole security deposit. Rather the leasing agent is obliged to determine a cost to repair the item. If this estimate is large enough to justify not returning the security deposit the renter should be informed of the estimated cost of repairing the apartment.

Is Your Apartment Clean Enough?

All apartments should be cleaned thoroughly before the tenant vacates the property. This should include extensive cleaning of all rooms of the apartment including the bedrooms, bathrooms and any common areas. A cleaning should also include cleaning of all of the blinds in the apartment. Blinds can be rather difficult to clean and many leasing agents charge approximately $10 per blind if they deem there is a need to clean these items. This can add up rather quickly if there are a number of windows in the apartment.

Many leasing agents also perform a number of standard cleaning functions when any resident vacates the property. This may include items such as cleaning out the refrigerator, shampooing the carpet or repainting the walls. When these items are required, there is typically a fee associated with each item. In many cases, adding up these required fees results in a number which is likely already approaching the sum of the security deposit. Additionally, leasing agents often only allow for one hour of cleaning services to prepare an apartment for the next residents. This is rarely enough time to complete the work and therefore renters wind up being charged an additional fee at an hourly rate.

Have You Read Your Contract Documents?

Renters who want to have the greatest chance of having a large portion of their security deposit refunded to them should be very familiar with their contract documents. This is important while living in the apartment as well as while getting ready to vacate the apartment. It is important to be familiar with the contract terms while living in the apartment because it can prevent the renter from making decorating choices which are explicitly prohibited by the rental agreement. These types of decisions can be costly in the long run because they may result in the renter being assessed for perceived damages by the leasing agent.

Renters should also carefully review the contract documents as they are preparing to vacate the property. This is important because it may help the renter to clean and make repairs to the apartment in accordance to guidelines set forth by the leasing agent. Doing this will make it much more likely the renter will not be assessed exorbitant fees at the conclusion of the rental agreement.

How Much Apartment Can You Afford?

Deciding how much apartment they can afford is one of the most important decisions a renter will have to make. This decision will help to determine a number of factors include the size and location of the potential apartment as well as the types of amenities offered. Those who are interested in renting an apartment will have to consider all of their current expenses in comparison to their monthly cash flow. They will also have to determine whether or not there are changes they can make to their current budget to make a larger or more well situated apartment affordable.

Consider All of Your Expenses

When deciding how much apartment they can afford, renters should carefully consider all of their monthly expenses in relation to their monthly income. Expenses may include, but are not limited to, utilities such as gas, water and electric, telephone, cell phone, Internet services, cable television, car insurance, renterís insurance, gas for car, cost of commuting to work, groceries and other incidental charges. Subtracting these costs from the monthly income will give the renter a good idea of how much money they can afford to spend on rent each month. Renters might also consider subtracting an additional amount out of their monthly income to give them the opportunity to save some money each month.

Expenses to be considered should also include expenses for entertainment purposes such as dining in restaurants, going to movie theaters or cultural events. Even movie rentals should be considered in this category. Considering these expenses is necessary because otherwise the renter may not allot a portion of their budget for such purposes and may find themselves unable to participate in some previously enjoyed leisure activities.

Is There Room for Improvement?

When examining the monthly budget, renter should take the opportunity to determine whether or not there is room for improvement in their current financial situation. For example a renter may find they are able to minimize their monthly bills by obtaining their car insurance and renterís insurance from the same insurance carrier. The carrier may be willing to offer a discount to a customer who utilizes their services for more than one type of insurance. Likewise there may be the opportunity to minimize expenses by bundling services such as telephone, Internet and possibly even cable television.

Also, consider entertainment expenses as an opportunity for financial improvement. If a renter currently eats out in restaurants for dinner on both Friday and Saturday of every week, they could consider limiting these dining experiences to only one night a week or even only one night every other week. This can result in a significant cost savings which may enable the renter to afford a more expensive apartment.

Other areas where renters can sometimes cut expenses are on cell phone bills and cable television bills. Examine your cell phone bill carefully. If you are not using all of your minutes each month, it might be worthwhile to switch to a plan with fewer minutes. This would lower your monthly bill without causing you to make any sacrifices. One area where sacrificing might contribute to more monthly cash flow is with cable television. Renters who pay higher fees for premium channels can consider eliminating these channels. All of these small changes to monthly spending can contribute to the renter being able to afford a more expensive apartment which may be larger or in a better location than the apartment they would be able to afford without making changes.

Is There a Need for Improvement?

Although trimming superfluous expenses is always a good financial strategy, renters should determine if this is necessary in terms of their rental situation before making drastic changes. Once a renter has established the amount of money they can afford to spend in rent, they can start to look for available apartments in that price range. If the renter is happy with the choices available to them at this time, there may not be a need to make financial adjustments at this time. However, if the renter is not happy with the options available, financial changes and stricter budgeting are warranted.

Maintenance on a Rental Property

Maintenance on a rental property can be a confusing issue. Renters may mistakenly assume all maintenance is the responsibility of the leasing agent and maintenance staff but this is usually not true. In many cases the leasing agent and maintenance staff are responsible for maintaining the common areas and performing major repairs on the apartments but the renters do typically have some responsibilities. These responsibilities are often defined in the rental agreement and the renter should familiarize himself with this document to verify his rights if a dispute arises.

Renter Responsibilities

Typically renters have the responsibility of maintaining their apartment and the surrounding area. This may include the interior of the apartment as well as deck or patio space. However, maintenance of these areas applies to generally cleanliness only and not issues such as painting or repairs to the exterior or the interior of the apartment structure or the appliances within the apartment.

Additionally, renters are responsible for small repairs in their home. This may include plunging a clogged toilet or changing a light bulb. However, if there are any duties a renter feels uncomfortable performing such as changing a light bulb in a high location, the renter should contact the maintenance staff for assistance.

Renters also have a responsibility to show common courtesy to other renters by not intentionally damaging or otherwise marring public areas. This includes vandalism, littering and even failure to pick up after dogs. Renters who fail to follow these rules of common courtesy may be subject to fines or other penalties according to the rental agreement.

Leasing Agent Responsibilities

The leasing agent and maintenance staff are generally held responsible for major items such as repairs to the exterior of the building, fixing appliances which are malfunctioning and dealing with plumbing issues such as leaky pipes. Additionally, the maintenance staff is responsible for intervening if the renter is having trouble with public utilities. Problem such as no hot water or heat to the apartment should be addressed by the maintenance staff in conjunction with the public utilities entity.

The leasing agent and maintenance staff is also responsible for maintaining the common areas. This may include keeping grassy areas manicured and other common areas looking clean and attractive.

When the Leasing Agent is Not Taking Responsibility

As previously discussed, the leasing agent has certain responsibilities to perform tasks and address concerns and complaints by the renters. However, when the leasing agent is not fulfilling these responsibilities it could create a harmful living environment for the renter. For example hot water is required to adequately clean dishes. This is why there should always be hot water to the apartment. Additionally, in severely cold weather the inability to heat the apartment due to faulty utilities or windows which are not properly sealed can create a hazardous condition for the renter.

Both of the examples mentioned above are situations in which the renter may put in a hazardous condition by the leasing agentís negligence. In these situations the renter should contact the Department of Housing to determine the proper cause of action to take in this situation.

In some cases the renter may be informed the alleged transgression by the leasing agent is not actually his responsibility. However, in other situations the renter may be informed that the actions of the leasing agent are a serious violation of the rental agreement. In either case, the representative can provide information on how to proceed to achieve the desired results.

Read Your Contract Carefully

Many renters barely even skim their rental agreement before signing their name at the bottom. Most renters are primarily concerned with the monthly charges, one time only fees, required deposits and other financial matters. Once they verify this information is accurate according to their conversations with the leasing agent, they often sign the agreement with no questions asked. This is a mistake because a rental agreement is a legal contract which may have a host of important information which the renter should be aware of before signing the document.

Considering a Roommate?

Those who are considering the possibility of a roommate may mistakenly believe this is possible because they are living alone and have two bedrooms and two bedrooms. These uninformed renters may see an opportunity to share their rent with another. However, some rental agreements strictly prohibit renters from soliciting their own roommates and allowing an additional person to move into the apartment after the lease is already signed. Renters who violate this agreement may face harsh penalties. These penalties may even include eviction.

Renters who want to have the option of a roommate should ideally make this decision before the contract is signed. This will enable the homeowner to put provisions into the contract to allow for the renter to add an additional resident at any time. The leasing agent may still require final approval of your roommate but this approval process will likely be dependent on the results of a background check as well as a check of the potential roommateís finances.

Want to Adopt a Pet?

Renters who wish to adopt a pet in the near future should also familiarize themselves with the rental agreement. This is important because restrictions on the types, size and specific breed of pets apply not only when the renter moves in but throughout the terms of his rental agreement. This means a renter who has signed contractual documents stating they do not own any of the prohibited pets such as dogs or cats are not free to purchase or adopt additional pets during the course of the rental agreement. Therefore, renters who do not have pets but plan to adopt or purchase pets in the near future should read the contract documents as if they are already a pet owner and decide whether or not to sign based on the statements within the policy.

Plan on Having Visitors Regularly?

Even renters who have regular overnight guests should familiarize themselves with their rental agreement before signing the document. This is important because frequent guests may actually be considered residents in some situations. This will likely depend on the specific rental agreement but it is not entirely uncommon for leasing agents to specify that visitors who spend a specific number of nights on the property per month are considered to be residents of the apartment. This is important because the rental agreement may clearly identify how many people may reside in the apartment at any one time.

Visitors who are staying at the apartment too often may put the resident at risk of being accused of having additional persons living in the apartment. In some situations this might be considered cause for eviction. For this reason, the renter should be sure he is familiar with the terms of the agreement before allowing others to spend the night in the apartment on a regular basis.

Rent to Own

Some potential homeowners who are not able to purchase a home right away consider rent to own options instead. A rent to own option, often referred to as a lease, is essentially a rental contract for the rental of a property which includes the stipulation that the renter will be given the option of purchasing the property at the conclusion of the lease. This type of rental agreement may not be worthwhile for all renters but there are some who will find this type of agreement to suit their needs quite well. In particular renters with bad credit who might be unable to buy a home otherwise and renters who aren't quite sure they really want to buy a home. It can also be a worthwhile agreement for homeowners who are planning to sell their home buy may not want to sell it immediately.

When Your Credit is Bad

Potential homeowners with bad credit may find a rent to own situation may be just what they are looking for to help them purchase their dream home. There are a variety of financing options currently available and it is likely even homeowners with poor credit can find a financing option but it is not likely this option will be favorable. Homeowners with poor credit are often shackled with unfavorable loan terms such as higher interest rates, requirements to pay points and adjustable rate mortgages instead of fixed rate mortgages. In these situations, it might be worthwhile for the renter to repair his credit before attempting to purchase a home.

One of the best ways to repair credit is to maintain good credit in the present and into the future. Most blemishes on credit reports are erased after a certain period of time. Renters who have poor credit can work on repaying their current debts in a timely fashion and with time their credit score will improve. During this time participating in a rent to own program allows the renter additional time to repair his credit and may also allow the renter to accumulate financial resources which will enable him to purchase the home when the lease period is over.

When You Just Arenít Ready to Buy a Home

Some renters opt for a rent to own program when they arenít quite sure they really want to own a home. In these types of agreements, renters are given the option of purchasing the home at the end of the agreement period but they are not obligated to purchase this home. This allows the renter to see what it is like to own a home without having to commit to homeownership.

Renters who are renting a home may learn a great deal about homeownership during the rental period. This may include information about maintaining the landscaping of the property and dealing with conflicts with neighbors. It may also entail caring for and maintaining a significantly larger domicile than most apartment renters have to maintain. Some renters are not quite sure they are ready to handle all of these issues and may use a rent to own agreement as a trial period to determine whether or not homeownership suits them.

When the Homeowner Just Isnít Ready to Sell

Some homeowners offer a rent to own option when they plan to sell their home but do not want to do so immediately. Some homeowners may be hoping for property values to rise before they sell their home so they can either regain the amount they have invested in the house or profit from the purchase price of the home. These homeowners might choose to rent out their home during this time and offer the renter the option of purchasing the house after a set time period. This enables the seller to earn an income from rent while they are no longer living in the home. The rent they charge to the renter is often enough to cover the mortgage and yield a profit making it a financially wise decision for the seller.

Rental Swaps

Some vacationers find a rental swap to be an ideal situation when they are traveling. Homeowners, especially in desired locations, may find there is a great deal of interest from others who would like to rent their home for a short period of time. Typically this is about one to three weeks although it may be longer or shorter in some cases. A rental swap is essentially where a homeowner in one location offers the use of their home to another homeowner in exchange for use of the other homeowners home. Ideally these swaps will take place concurrently but in some situations swaps are organized at different times of the year.

A Rental Swap Saves You Money

For many a rental swap is worth considering because it can result in a tremendous financial savings. Lodging often accounts for a large portion of a vacationers travel expenses. By eliminating these costs the vacationer may find they are able to add additional aspects to their vacation. For example, by eliminating lodging costs, a vacationer may have money left over in the travel budget to see a few plays, eat dinner at extravagant restaurants or purchase tickets to sporting events.

A rental swap, however, does not always automatically translate to a financial savings. Consider the cost of staying in a hotel within walking distance to major attractions as opposed to participating in a rental swap 10-20 miles away from most major attractions. In the case of the rental swap, the vacationer will most likely have to rent a car during their stay but might not have to do so when staying in a hotel. The need for a car, whether or not the kitchen in a rental swap will be utilized to cook meals and other factors should be considered in determining whether a rental swap or hotel stay is more financially logical.

A Rental Swap is More Comfortable than a Hotel

In most cases a rental swap usually results in a more comfortable stay than a visit to a hotel. Of course there will always be situations in which the quality and even the size of the hotel may be superior to the conditions of the rental shop but for the most part, vacationers usually feel more comfortable in a rental swap situation. Staying in a home typically provides the vacationer with more privacy as well as the ability to spread out a little more. This can be very beneficial for keeping the peace especially for large families who may quickly feel overcrowded in a hotel situation.

There are Risks to a Rental Swap

While a rental swap may certainly seem appealing, there are some inherent risks to this type of lodging situation. First of all the possibility of the rental property not being exactly as described is a very real risk. Homeowners may exaggerate the appeal of their property either intentionally or unintentionally. Regardless of the intent of the homeowner, the vacationer may still find themselves in a situation where they are disappointed with the accommodations. This may be because the house is not as large or well appointed as described or because the house is older and less well maintained than depicted.

Another risk to a rental shop is the possibility of the other homeowner not noting the correct dates. Although this is also a possibility with a hotel, it can be more troubling when the vacationer was counting on the rental swap for their accommodations during the stay. While a hotel might make every effort to accommodate the hotel guests when there is a mistake, homeowners in a rental swap may not have the available resources to find an alternate place for the vacationers to stay.

One final risk which exists in a rental swap, is potential damage to your own property when you allow others to use the property. Homeowners can work to minimize the trouble in these situations by screening those who they are considering for a rental swap carefully. Additionally, homeowners can take security measures by alerting the police as well as neighbors that a stranger will be staying in the home. This will help everyone to be more vigilant and aware of the potential for problems.

Renting with Dogs

Renters who have a dog or more than one dog may face additional challenges when renting an apartment or a house. One of the primary challenges the renters may face is finding a living situation which is acceptable to them and also willing to accept their pets. This can be difficult as many rental properties do not allow dogs at all. Those who do allow animals on the property may place certain restrictions on they size and breed of dog which may reside on the property.

Finding an Acceptable Living Situation

The first step in renting with dogs is to find an acceptable living situation. For those who wish to rent with dogs, the first question to be asked should be whether or not dogs are allowed to live on the property. This is important because it can save the renter a great deal of time. The renter may otherwise invest a great deal of time learning more about the property or even undergoing a credit check only to find out pet are not permitted.

For some dog owners, finding a rental situation which allows dogs is not the end of the search. The renter should also confirm the type of dog he owns will be allowed to live on the property. This may include both the size of the dog as well as the breed as some apartment complexes place limitations on the size of the dog and also prohibit certain breeds. Again confirming these facts early in the search for an apartment can be a tremendous time savings especially for those who own large or commonly banned breeds.

Renters should also consider the surrounding area when selecting a rental property. An ideal location would be one in which there is an adequate location to walk and exercise the dogs. Areas with large grassy areas may be ideal while areas which do not have a location to walk a dog may be problematic.

Read Contracts Carefully

Renters who have dogs should read their contract carefully before making a decision to rent a particular property. This is important because many landlords may impose restrictions on renters who own dogs. These restrictions may include, but are not limited to, requiring an additional security deposit for the renter, requiring specific cleaning methods on the carpets after the renter vacates the apartment and holding the renter responsible if the dog engages in nuisance barking. Nuisance barking can be a problem in apartment situations where the apartments are located close together and even share a common wall. Renters should be aware that in some situations, nuisance barking can be a cause for eviction. For these reasons, renters who own dogs should take the time to familiarize themselves with the rental contract.

Take Care of Your Rental Property

Finally, renters who have dogs may have to take additional efforts to maintain their apartment. This may include more diligent cleaning, especially of the carpets. Renters with dogs should respond quickly to accidents in the house to minimize the possibility of permanent staining and odors. Each accident should be addressed immediately and every effort should be made to clean the affected area completely.

Renters with dogs should also vacuum regularly especially if their dog is a heavy shedder. This will help to keep the living environment cleaner and will also minimize the amount of cleaning required when the renter vacates the property. Regularly vacuuming will prevent hair from being embedded into the carpet so deeply that it is difficult to remove.

Finally, renters with dogs should take care to pick up after their dogs while on walks and to keep their dogs leashed while in common areas. Many cities have leash laws and laws regarding picking up after dogs. Even if these laws are not in effect, renters should follow these policies as a courtesy to their neighbors. Additionally, keeping dogs on leashes during walks helps to ensure their safety by preventing them from running into the street.

Saving Money by Renting

For many renters the possibility of using a rental situation to save money is a foreign idea. These renters often bemoan the fact that they have to rent a property rather than purchase a property because they feel as though not owning the property is basically throwing money away each month. However, this is not entirely true. While there are certainly benefits to homeownership and building equity homeowners can also benefit financially by renting an apartment rather than purchasing a home.

While it is certainly true that money spent each month on rent does not get the renter any closer to homeownership while each monthly mortgage payment makes the homeowner one step closer to owning the property completely. However, this is not the whole story. Renters should also consider the amount of money they will be able to save annually for the purpose of purchasing a home by living in a rental property right now.

A Smaller Apartment Can Lead to a Bigger House

Some would be homeowners find renting a small apartment can allow them to start saving for the purpose of purchasing a house in the future. Renters who are willing to sacrifice comfort now and stay in the smallest apartment possible will likely be able to save the most money towards purchasing a home.

In general the monthly rent for an apartment is based on a value per square foot. This value may vary slightly from one property to the next but is likely to be very similar in properties in the same general area. This means apartments which are smaller in terms of square footage are likely to be less expensive overall. Therefore renters who would normally feel more comfortable and able to spread out might opt for a smaller apartment just so they can begin saving more money for their home purchase.

Budget Wisely to Save Money

Renters who want to save money for the purchase of a home while renting an apartment should understand their monthly rent is not the only factor which may prevent them from saving money while they rent. For example entertainment costs should carefully be considered when a renter is trying to save money. Most rental properties have a fully equipped kitchen making it ideal for the renter to prepare meals at home as opposed to going out to eat. Renters who cut down on eating dinner out may find they are able to save quite a bit of money each year.

Likewise renters who are spending an excess amount of money on superfluous items may have difficulty saving for a house while renting an apartment. Examining all current monthly expenditures can help the renter to determine where there is the potential for financial savings. Making changes such as debt consolidation may be one way to decrease monthly bills but this is certainly not the only solution. Renters can make other changes such as canceling subscriptions to premium movie channels, minimizing cell phone plans to include only the amount of minutes used each month and making changes to insurance plans to result in an overall savings. Changes to insurance plans may include having your car and renterís insurance covered by the same carrier. Many carriers offer discounted services to renters who are willing to bundle their services. All of these slight changes can help to enable a renter to save money for a home purchase in the future.

Sharing a Rental with a Roommate

Sharing a rental property, whether it is an apartment or a house, can be either a dream come true or a living nightmare. There are many advantages to having a roommate; however, there are also disadvantages. When these disadvantages are severe they can result in an uncomfortable living environment in some situations and even a dangerous living environment in other situations. There are a couple of ways a renter can protect themselves when sharing their rental property with a roommate. This includes screening the potential roommate carefully and including the roommate on the rental agreement.

The Advantages and Disadvantages to Having a Roommate

Having a roommate can certainly be advantageous in some situations. The primary advantage is financial. Renters who opt to have a roommate, essentially cut their rent in half if they opt to have one roommate or in thirds if they opt to have two roommates. This is ideal for renters who would like to have a larger apartment but would not be able to afford such an apartment without the assistance of a roommate.

Another advantage to having a roommate is the opportunity to share household responsibilities with the roommate. Of course this is only an advantage when the roommate is willing to do his share of the work on a regular basis. If this is not the case, it may result in a huge disadvantage which will be covered briefly in the section on disadvantages.

One of the most significant disadvantages to having a roommate is a lack of privacy. Those who live alone do not ever have to worry about not having time to themselves while they are in their apartment. However, when a renter has a roommate, there is no guarantee the renter will ever have any time to himself while he is in the apartment.

Another disadvantage to having a roommate is the distribution of household responsibilities may not always be even. Roommates should have a discussion regarding the household responsibilities such as cleaning the common areas but there is always the possibility that one roommate may not do his share of the work. When this happens it can create conflict and resentment among the roommates. This conflict can make the living situation quite uncomfortable.

Select a Compatible Roommate

When selecting a roommate, the renter should be careful to select a compatible roommate. In the previous section we discussed how conflicts can arise when one roommate does not do his share of the cleaning. However, incompatible cleaning styles are only a small portion of the compatibility issues roommates may face. One important issue is entertaining. If one roommate has visitors at the apartment often, it can cause problems if the other roommate is not comfortable with this.

Even the times in which the roommates normally sleep can cause problems. If one roommate goes to bed early and wakes up at 4:00 am, it can be problematic if the other roommate likes to stay up late and not wake up until 9:00 am. In this case the roommates may not only begin to get on each otherís nerves but they may also begin to adversely affect the otherís job or social life.

Include the Roommate on the Rental Agreement

Finally, renters should be sure to include their roommate or roommates on the rental agreement. This is very important because it helps to protect all of the roommates. Inclusion of all of the roommates prevents one roommate from being able to ask another to leave unjustly. This may occur when conflicts arise but inclusion on the rental agreement ensures each of the roommates has a right to live on the property. Placing each of the roommatesí names on the rental agreement also prevents one roommate from not making their rent payments in a timely manner. It will also help to prevent one roommate from being held legally responsible for not paying the rent on time by the leasing agent.

Should You Rent A House Or An Apartment?

Deciding whether to rent an apartment or a house can be a very difficult decision for some renters. There are certain advantages and disadvantages to each option. The renter should carefully consider these points when making his decision. Whether or not an apartment rental or a home rental is ideal for a particular renter will largely depend on his personal preference as well as his current needs in a living situation. For some renting an apartment is perfect while others find a home rental meets their needs best. This article will examine the advantages and disadvantages of each situation to help readers make a more informed decision regarding the type of rental situation which may be beneficial to them.

The Advantages and Disadvantages of Renting a House

There are many advantages to renting a house as opposed to an apartment. One of the primary advantages is this situation affords renters who would normally be unable to afford to purchase a house the opportunity to live in a house for a much more affordable price. Another advantage to renting a house is it may offer the renter many more options. Apartments are usually pretty standard in terms of size, number of bedrooms and number of bathrooms. Renters who have specific needs such as five bathrooms and three bedrooms may have a difficult time finding an apartment with these specifications but may find rental homes which offer these options.

Location is often another advantage associated with renting a house. Apartments are usually situated in more commercial areas while houses available for rent can usually be found in more residential areas. Many renters favor this situation because it makes their rental property feel more secluded. Many house rentals also include a backyard which is desirable for renters with children or pets.

One of the major disadvantages to renting a house, is there may not be a great deal of certainty regarding the amount of time the renter will be allowed to rent the house. While a contract may protect the rights of the renter for a certain period of time, there are no guarantees the homeowner will extend the contract beyond the existing terms. This means as the contract is due to expire; the renter may be given notice that the house would not be available for rent in the future.

Conversely, this situation is rare in apartments and most renters are confident there will be the opportunity to renew their lease each time it expires.

The Advantages and Disadvantages of Renting an Apartment

Perhaps one of the most significant advantages of renting an apartment is the amenities which are often available when renting an apartment in an apartment complex as opposed to renting a home or even renting an apartment in a private home. Amenities such as pools, hot tubs, exercise rooms, saunas, meeting rooms and theaters are just a few of the amenities often offered when renting an apartment.

Affordability is another advantage to renting an apartment. Rent for an apartment is usually significantly lower than rent for a house. Although the apartment may be significantly smaller than the house, many renters find they are only able to afford these options.

A lack of privacy may be one of the most significant disadvantages to renting an apartment. Apartments are usually situated fairly closely together and most apartments usually share a common wall with one of their neighbors. Renters may find their neighbors end up knowing a great deal more about them than they had intended simply because the living situation makes it difficult to keep one's life private.

Having to contend with noisy neighbors is another downfall to renting an apartment. As previously, mentioned apartments often share a common wall with a neighbor. As a result renters may run the risk of having noisy neighbors who listen to loud music or have boisterous friends visiting late at night.

Vacation Rentals

Many vacationers opt to rent a home in their vacation destination rather than staying in a hotel. For these vacationers, this is a worthwhile option because it gives the vacationer a more comfortable place to stay with features such as cooking facilities which are not typically offered in commercial hotels. Finding these vacation rentals can be significantly more difficult than simply making hotel reservations but many vacationers report this to be a worthwhile effort. However, some care should be taken when renting a vacation home to ensure the quality of the home meets the expectations of the vacationers.

Finding Vacation Rentals

Finding a vacation rental property can obviously be much more difficult than simply renting a hotel during the vacation. Of course some vacationers will be lucky and have a friend or family member who owns a home in a particular vacation destination and is willing to rent it out to others. Those who do not have this type of fortunate situation have other options for finding a vacation rental property.

Many homeowners in popular vacation destinations rent out their home during the peak season. These homeowners may allow a realtor to handle the transactions. Contacting realtors in the area of the vacation destination and inquiring about available rental properties in the area is one way to start the search. The realtor will likely be able to assist you in finding a home for rent.

There are also many popular websites where homes for rent are listed directly by the owner of the home. Searching the Internet can lead you to a reliable source of homes for rent. These homes are usually divided into categories by region and will likely provide you instant access to available dates. It will likely give useful information such as whether or not pets are allowed, the number of bedrooms and bathrooms as well as the size of the home and the proximity to nearby attraction. The listing may also provide useful information regarding the furnishings of the home. Some rental properties may include items such as bedding and cookware while some may not.

Ask Questions before Renting a Vacation Home

Vacationers who wish to rent a vacation home as opposed to spending their vacation in a hotel should exercise a certain amount of caution in selecting a property to rent. Being cautious will not only enable the vacationer to ensure his rental property meets his expectations but will also help to avoid potentially dangerous situations. One way to avoid these potential problems is by asking a great deal of questions during the process.

Renting a vacation home through a rental agency is ideal for safety purposes. In these situations the agency handles the entire rental giving the renter the security of knowing they are not walking into a potentially dangerous situation. However, even in this situation the renter should ask some important questions. These questions will be explained in the subsequent paragraphs.

How old is the property? Potential renters should ask questions about the age of the property and whether or not appliances, plumbing and electricity have been updated. This is important because this type of information can mean the difference between a comfortable stay in the property and dealing with problems related to the age of the home.

What is included in the rental? While most rentals include the basic necessities, there are some rental agreements which only include the use of the house and furniture. Renters may be required to bring along bedding, towels and even cookware.

How often is the property rented and how is it maintained? These two questions are inter-related because properties which are rented often see significantly more wear and tear than properties which are only rented a couple of times per year. Properties which are rented often should employ a maid service to clean the property thoroughly between each rental and possibly during longer rental periods.

What is the exact location of the property? Asking this question will enable the vacationer to determine whether or not the property is ideally situated for the purposes of the vacation. For example a vacationer on a ski trip would want to be situated close to the mountains while a vacationer more interested in a cultural vacation might be interested in a downtown location which will likely be closer to museums and other locations of interest.

What Does the Rent Include?

There is no simple answer to the question of what is included in the rent. This is because the answer will likely vary from one apartment complex to the next. Some apartment complexes may include a variety of items within their rent while others may charge renters additional fees as needed and still others may require the renters to register directly with individual public utilities and handle these expenses on their own.

Likewise some apartment complexes may include additional features with the price of the rent while others may charge additional fees for these features. A pool, exercise room, meeting room or theater are just a few examples which may be offered by an apartment complex. In most cases the use of these amenities are included in the price of the rent but there are exceptions where the renter is charged an additional fee for the privilege of using these amenities.

Consider the Price of Utilities

When considering the price or a rental property, the renter should first determine whether or not utilities are included in the cost of the rent. This is significant because depending on the size of the property and the climate of the area, heating and cooling costs can be rather expensive. In most cases, the renter is responsible for the cost of their own utilities and their apartment is individually monitored for usage and the renter is billed monthly by the utility company. However, in the case of an individual renting an apartment in a private home as opposed to an apartment complex, the homeowner may collect money for utility uses in another way. Depending on the agreement between the homeowner and the renter the monthly rent may be set at a rate which includes a contribution to the utility costs or the renter may be assessed a pre-determined percentage of each utility bill on a monthly basis.

It is important to consider the price of utilities when they are not included in the rent because failure to do so can lead to unpleasant surprises in the future. For example a renter in a particularly cold climate may rent a spacious apartment for a great rate only to find out later that the cost of heating the apartment makes it difficult for the renter to afford to live in the apartment.

Consider Amenities which are ìFreeî

When renters are selecting an apartment, they should consider the amenities which are ìfreeî as opposed to the amenities for which the renter is charged an additional fee. The word free is used in quotations in the heading of this section to indicate these amenities do not always come without a price. A renter may not pay a usage fee for some amenities but it is very likely the privilege of using these amenities is factored into the monthly rent.

As an example consider two 800 square foot apartments in the same geographical area. Each apartment may have a similar layout and comparable square footage but the monthly rents associated with these two apartments might be quite different. In examining the amenities you might notice the higher prices apartment has access to a pool, an exercise room and a theater all for the use of residents while the lower priced apartment offers no such amenities. In this case the residents of the more expensive apartments are actually paying a higher monthly rent as a result of the amenities offered.

In a case such as the example above, renters should weight their options carefully. If they can afford to pay the more expensive rent, they should carefully consider whether or not they wish to pay a higher fee for use of the amenities. A renter who doesnít like to swim, belongs to a gym and does not have a great deal of free time to watch movies may decide they would be better off selecting the lower priced apartment without amenities.

CPSIA information can be obtained
at www.ICGtesting.com
Printed in the USA
BVHW041351121120
593173BV00007B/175